Royal Doulton Figurines and Character Jugs

Katharine Morrison McClinton

Wallace-Homestead
Book Company

Royal Doulton
Figurines and Character Jugs
Copyright 1978 Katharine Morrison McClinton

Third Printing, 1979

ISBN 0-87069-210-0
Library of Congress Catalog
76-24195

Published By

Wallace-Homestead Book Co.
1912 Grand Avenue
Des Moines, Iowa 50305

Contents

Preface

During the past few years Royal Doulton Character Jugs and bone china figurines have become the craze of a large number of enthusiastic antiques collectors. This is evidenced not only by the advertisements in such magazines as *Hobbies, Spinning Wheel* and *Antique Trader,* but also by the vast number of letters of inquiry received by the Doulton Company. Royal Doulton is a rapidly growing field of collecting, and prices are mounting day by day. Character Jug collectors have become history buffs and Dickens enthusiasts, and a large number of women see themselves in the enchanting figures of such models as Sunday Morn or Summer's Day. Also, collectors who were first attracted by the quaintness of the dainty figurines or the striking caricatures of the Character Jugs are now asking specific questions about the marks, dates, artists, and the technicalities of the production.

This book is written to answer some of these questions. However, there is still considerable lack of information available because of incomplete factory records due to loss by fire or other mishaps. The Character Jugs and figurines were only a small part of the output of the Doulton Company. They were aimed at a popular market and, in the beginning, probably not sufficiently valued. Now these articles have become an important part of the production of the Doulton factory.

It is hoped that this book will supply some answers to the questions of today's collectors.

Acknowledgments

I wish to thank the following collectors and dealers for their valuable assistance. This book could not have been written without the cooperation of Susan Kasulka and Mr. and Mrs. Robert M. Fortune. I also wish to thank Mrs. Ann Cook for information about her dog collection; Mrs. Crayton K. Black, Richard Wright, Ron Heberlee, D. Shiaras, Martha Laestar, and Wanda Wempe.

In addition to the study of the figures themselves, the various catalogs and brochures issued by the Doulton Company through the years have been an especially valuable source of information. Although few of these catalogs are dated or in color, a careful study produced considerable information.

I. The Royal Doulton Potteries

Royal Doulton is one of the best known manufacturers of china and earthenware today. Thousands of people own sets of modern Royal Doulton or fine bone china, but few know the wide range of products made by the Doulton potteries over the space of two centuries of their operation. From its beginnings in 1815 to the present day, Doulton has produced a line of fine art products along with numerous popular wares such as Toby and Character Jugs and figures. All of these products are available to antiques collectors today, and they are especially desirable because of their comparatively low prices and because the Doulton system of marking gives authenticity to each piece.

There were two Doulton potteries, Lambeth and Burslem. The Lambeth pottery was located at Lambeth near London and the Burslem pottery was at Burslem in Staffordshire. The wares at each pottery were different from those of the other.

The Doulton Pottery at Lambeth, founded in 1815 by John Doulton, was primarily a stoneware pottery specializing in commercial and industrial stonewares, terra-cotta ale and porter bottles, covered jars, garden vases, statues, fountains, and all kinds of architectural work. Soon after the founding John Doulton was joined by John Watts and the firm became Doulton & Watts. From 1820 to 1854 the Doulton Pottery at Lambeth traded as Doulton & Watts. Besides utilitarian wares Doulton & Watts also manufactured spirit flasks, busts, and heads of popular interest. Other miscellaneous products included whistles with dog heads, bird whistles, and banks in the shape of houses. Toby jugs were also early products. These were of conventional shape decorated with applied reliefs depicting topers with foaming tankards, stags, dogs, horsemen, birds, cottages, and windmills. The Punch and Dog Toby was made in about 1846 and is an early, valuable piece. So great was the demand for these Toby Philpots that Doulton continued to produce them until the Lambeth Works closed in 1956.

In 1877 Doulton & Company made a connection with Messrs. Pinter, Bourne & Company for the production of higher class wares in their Nile Street Pottery at Burslem, Staffordshire. This pottery was taken over completely by Doulton in 1881. When Doulton first made the connection, Burslem factory employed 160 workers, but by 1889 there were 1,200. The works at Burslem were quite distinct from those at Lambeth. Instead of stoneware, the production consisted mainly of fine porcelain.

The Burslem Pottery productions followed the lines of other high class firms, and the porcelain was of the finest quality. The decoration consisted of flower, landscape, and figure painting on vases, and elaborate service plates and game and dessert plates with gilding and rich coloring.

Wall masks by Richard Garbe. Left, FATE, porcelain with ivory glaze. Burslem script marks, 10½ inches, edition 100. Right, ST. AGNES, porcelain mask with turquoise. Burslem script marks. (Courtesy Richard Dennis from illustration in Doulton Pottery catalogue of an exhibition of pottery at The Fine Arts Society, London, June-July 1975.)

SPRING by Richard Garbe A.R.A. Tinted matt glaze, 18 inches high. c. 1933.

Mark on base of figure. (Collection Susan Kasulka.)

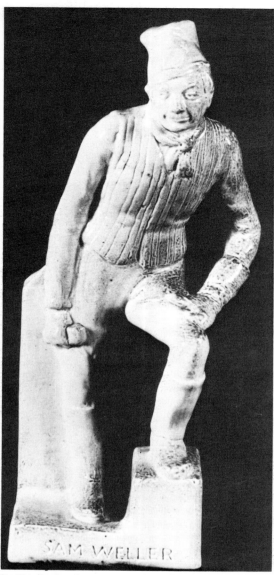

Buff, salt-glazed stoneware figure of Sam Weller modeled by Leslie Harradine c. 1912. (Courtesy Doulton & Co., Ltd.)

Fine, hand-painted porcelain vases were made for exhibitions and gold-embellished services were made for the trade. Burslem also produced simply decorated and comparatively inexpensive earthenware tablewares. A large section of the factory was also devoted to producing china and earthenware lamps and toilet sets.

Expensive tableware and large, elaborate vases were especially popular in the period at the end of the nineteenth century. Henry Doulton was anxious to have his factory compete in this type of expensive china, so he began to gather a group of designers, painters, gilders, etchers, and modelers to meet the demand and to compete with the other English and Continental factories of the time.

The staff of accomplished artists already at Burslem included painters of flowers, fish, game, and landscapes, as well as those who specialized in gilding. To these Doulton now added artists obtained from other factories such as Worcester, Minton, Coalport, Cauldron, Copeland, and even Sevres. Never before had such a gifted group of artists come together in one factory.

The first large display of Doulton's china was shown at the World's Columbian Exposition at Chicago in 1893. Among the exhibits were vases made at Burslem especially for the exhibition, such as the Columbian vase which was modeled by Charles J. Noke and painted by Charles Labarre of Sevres. Other vases, including four Diana vases, were also modeled by Noke.

Charles J. Noke was one of the most important workers at the Burslem plant. Noke had joined the Burslem Pottery in 1889. Noke was a talented modeler. He had received his training at Worcester. His forte was in the combination of color decoration with shape and line. Noke first modeled his subject in low relief. The form was brought out by the use of underglaze color and enamels; gold ornamentation added to the richness. By 1894, Noke had begun to model figures. His early figures included Ellen Terry as Queen Catherine, Sir Henry Irving as Cardinal Wolsey, Mephistopheles, and Marguerite and Doris Keane as Cavallini. In 1897 the Moorish Minstrel, Columbus, and the Jester had been produced. These figures were in large sizes, from 10 to 20 inches high, and few copies were made, except for a smaller Jester. The figures were made of a Parian-like clay and were very different from the later figures of earthenware or bone china which are so much in demand with collectors today.

At the turn of the century, Doulton introduced a group of wares that were allied with the arts and crafts movement. Among these was Holbein Ware which was introduced by Noke at Doulton, Burslem, in 1895. This ware had realistic or stylized heads or scenes in the manner of the artist Holbein. The pattern was modeled in relief, and a special glaze gave an uneven, rough texture. A few years later, in 1898, Charles Noke introduced Rembrandt Ware, a rough-textured, rugged looking ware made of ordinary clay fired at a low heat. Still another ware introduced by Noke was Morrisian Ware in 1901. The designs on this ware included dancing figures with wreaths and stylized flowers in hues of red, yellow, and brown. The ware has its own special mark. Mandarin Ware was advertised in 1905. The shapes were Oriental and the designs included birds of bright plumage upon a ground of "Imperial Yellow."

The popular series wares such as Dickensware, Jackdaw of Rheims, Shakespeare Ware, Coaching Days, Canterbury Pilgrims, King Arthur's Knights, Sailing Ships, and many others were first introduced in the early 1900s and remained popular through the 1920s when they were discontinued. These wares were made in complete luncheon and dinner sets as well as tobacco jars and candlesticks.

Perhaps the most important ware introduced by Noke was Rouge Flambé, a re-creation of the transmutation glazes of the Chinese master potters of the Sung, Ming, and early Ch'ing dynasties. Noke experimented with these glazes for many years before he introduced them to the public.

The first exhibition of Rouge Flambé was at the St. Louis Exposition in 1904. Noke continued to experiment with transmutation glazes and produced the Sung and Chang wares in the 1920s. There were vases with floral and landscape scenes and figures of animals, birds, and fish. During World War I, Noke developed Titanian Ware, a ware with a glaze similar to the finest Oriental porcelain. Designs of sea gulls, flowers, and cirrus clouds are seen through foggy mists of blues and greens. Titanian Ware was not produced in large quantities and was discontinued in 1929.

Through the years there has been an immense production of table-wares at the Burslem Doulton factory. In addition to the series wares, which were of earthenware decorated in underglaze colors and conceived in popular style for mass production, fine bone china was made in elaborate designs ornamented in gold.

The figures and Character Jugs that are the subject of this book were nearly all made at the Burslem factory. Charles J. Noke had become art director at Burslem in 1914. In addition to all the other wares that Noke introduced at Burslem, his interest in the 1920s and 1930s seemed to center on the Character Jugs and the bone china figurines, and they became some of the most popular and most successful products made at Burslem. Today these jugs and figures have become the craze with thousands of collectors, and they rank high on the list of most popular items in the collecting field.

Many salt-glazed figures and animal models made at Lambeth are quite popular with British collectors. However, although they were produced until the factory closed in 1956, they are not so well known to American collectors. Among the artists who modeled figures at Lambeth were John Broad, George Tinworth, Leslie Harradine, Richard Garbe, and Agnete Hoy who is well known for her figures of cats.

Cat, stoneware. Agnete Hoy. c.1956. Rare.

II. Royal Doulton Figurines

Royal Doulton figures were produced from the early days of the factory at Lambeth. John Broad modeled the terra-cotta figure The Lambeth Potter that Doulton produced at Lambeth in 1885, and in 1902 he modeled The Boer War Soldier. Charles J. Noke also modeled a few figures that were reproduced in the late nineteenth century, but these figures were all too large and too expensive for popular sales.

The figurines that are so popular with collectors today were manufactured at the Burslem factory. They were introduced by Charles J. Noke, the important modeler and designer. Noke had been interested in the old Staffordshire figures for many years, and he longed to revive their manufacture. Between 1909 and 1914 Noke commissioned a number of small figures, 7 to 9½ inches high, from designs by well-known sculptors of the period, which were reproduced by Doulton. Noke himself modeled some animals and two figures, The Dunce and Jester. None of the figures received popular acceptance except Darling, a small boy in a long nightgown, which was admired and purchased by Queen Mary. Under Noke's direction, many figures were produced between 1914 and 1920, including Jack Point, A Spook, Double Spook, and the figures from *The Beggar's Opera* and *Ali Baba and the Forty Thieves*.

In 1920 a group of Royal Doulton figures was shown at the British Industries Fair. In addition to earlier figures, the subjects included in the exhibit were The Mermaid, The Chelsea Pair, The Parson's Daughter, The Shepherd, and The Shepherdess. The excellent notice received encouraged Doulton to continue the production of figures of this type, and thus began the renaissance of figures of Staffordshire-type at Doulton's Burslem factory. Between 1920 and 1924 there were other figures produced, including figures from *The Mikado;* Pierrette, Harlequinade, The Proposal, and The Victorian Lady. An early catalog put out at about this time illustrates Fruit Gathering, a figure of a girl with a basket of fruit and a figure of a lamb at her side and The Goose Girl, a figure of a girl carrying a basket and a goose. Also illustrated were figures of Marie with powdered wig and bouffant skirt, Katherine, and Puff and Powder in wig and bouffant costume. Small Dickens figures, both 4 inches and 7 inches, were also illustrated. There was also mention of both The Forty Thieves series and The Beggar's Opera series. Other early figures include Motherhood, Pedlar Wolf, and Charley's Aunt from the play of that name written in the 1890s. A group of early children's figures included Child and Crab, The Land of Nod, The Little Land, Shy Anne, The Sleepy Scholar, The Diligent Scholar, Child Resting Under a Gooseberry Bush, and Upon Her Cheeks She Wept.

By 1924 Royal Doulton figures were becoming popular throughout the world. Noke had succeeded in establishing a new type of figure which retained the best of the Staffordshire tradition, but also borrowed some of the characteristics of the finer Chelsea figures and even drew influence from Sevres and Dresden. There was a large studio of artists at Burslem working with Noke and each designer's individual ideas produced a great variety in the figures. The artists included Leslie Harradine and Harry Tittensor. The workmen also included sculptors, potters, and painters of skill and dedication who worked together to produce figures that had simplicity of line and harmony of color combined with natural poses and facial expressions. To obtain these results five or more firings, one for each color, were necessary. The molding and casting were done in sections which were carefully welded together. This was followed by the initial firing. The figure was then hand-dipped in glaze and, after drying, was re-fired to give it sheen. Finally, the artist painted the figure with ceramic pigment, which fixed the colors for further firings.

The subjects of Doulton figurines range from artistic poses of the human figure in the nude, such as Dawn and Celia, done in hard bisque porcelain, to portrayals of characters from the works and plays of famous authors done in soft-paste porcelain and finished in colors. Altogether, more than 2,000 different figures have been produced, but, although new designs are added each year, some of the older ones are discontinued so that there are not more than 200 in current production. Through the years the subjects of figures have been so varied that there are categories to please the tastes of all sorts of collectors. The older figures are now becoming hard to find, and many of the discontinued figures are rare and expensive. For the collector this adds interest and excitement to the quest, as well as increase in the value of a collection.

Among the different categories of figures available to today's collectors are figures from Shakespeare, including Falstaff from *The Merry Wives of Windsor* and Miranda from *The Tempest*.

There are early (before 1925) figures of Ko-Ko and Yum-Yum from Gilbert and Sullivan's *The Mikado* and there are figures of Baba, Cassim and the Forty Thieves from *Ali Baba and the Forty Thieves*. The series of figures from John Gay's *Beggar's Opera* includes Polly Peachum, Macheath, The Highwayman, and The Beggar. Kate Hardcastle from Oliver Goldsmith's *She Stoops to Conquer* was a favorite figure which was first produced c. 1935 in pink and green and in red and green. It was popular for a number of years until it was discontinued c. 1951-1953.

In 1948 Royal Doulton produced a series of Period Figures in English History between 1080 and 1860. The figures were made of bone china and are from 10 to 11 inches high. They include Henrietta Maria, Queen of Charles I, HN 2005; The Lady Anne Nevill, Queen of Richard III, HN 2006; Mrs. Fitzherbert, the wife of George IV, HN 2007; Philippa of Hainault, Queen of Edward III, HN 2008; Eleanor of Provence, Queen of Henry III, HN 2009; The Young Miss Nightingale, HN 2011; and Margaret of Anjou, Queen of Henry VI, HN 2012. Doulton put out a catalog with historical notes and an illustration of each figure; however, the figures were not very popular and were discontinued in 1951-53. The most decorative figure of the group is The Lady Anne Nevill. She is depicted with medieval headdress and wears an ermine-trimmed robe. All of these figures are extremely rare today. The series was also produced in earthenware.

Popular figures from the London streets are some of the figurines most in demand today. These include The Lavender Woman, The Orange Lady, The Old Balloon Seller, The Flower Seller, Silks and Ribbons, Pearly Boy, and Pearly Girl.

Doulton produced four different balloon figures. The earliest figure, HN 583, 9 inches high, was The Balloon Seller. It is a standing figure of a woman wearing a hat and shawl and holding a baby in her arms which

BATHER, HN 687, "Potted," c.1928. White, nude body, dark blue cape with white design. (Collection Mr. & Mrs. Robert M. Fortune.)

MERMAID, HN 97. Nude with blonde hair, red beads, green tail, sitting on tan base. Pearlized. (Collection Mr. & Mrs. Robert M. Fortune.)

Period Figures
In English History

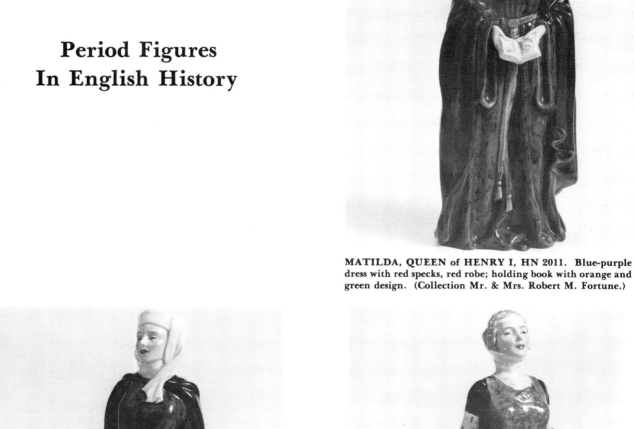

MATILDA, QUEEN of HENRY I, HN 2011. Blue-purple dress with red specks, red robe; holding book with orange and green design. (Collection Mr. & Mrs. Robert M. Fortune.)

ELEANOR of PROVENCE, QUEEN OF HENRY III. HN 2009. Purple-blue dress with flecks of red; red cape and shoes, white hat. (Collection Mr. & Mrs. Robert M. Fortune.)

PHILIPPA of HAINAULT, QUEEN of EDWARD III, HN 2008. Blue dress with red sleeves, green belt and pin, white armbands with black specks. Blonde hair. (Collection Mr. & Mrs. Robert M. Fortune.)

MARGARET of ANJOU, QUEEN of HENRY VI, HN 2012.
Blue-green dress with white border, orange base, yellow hat,
blonde hair. (Collection Mr. & Mrs. Robert M. Fortune.)

HENRIETTA MARIE, QUEEN of CHARLES I, HN 2005.
Full-skirted red dress and shoes, long coat of yellow and green
with blue flowers. Orange necklace, pin with blue center,
white earrings, dark brown hair. (Collection Mr. & Mrs.
Robert M. Fortune.)

MRS. FITZHERBERT, HN 2007. Cap and underskirt
white; cap with blue bows, yellow overskirt with rose and blue
flowers, red vest and fan with red handle. (Collection Mr. &
Mrs. Robert M. Fortune.)

THE YOUNG MISS NIGHTINGALE, HN 2010. Red
sleeveless coat, shoes, and feather on hat. Green skirt with
light green ruffle and purse; yellow umbrella with red trim.
(Collection Mr. & Mrs. Robert M. Fortune.)

LAVENDER WOMAN, HN 569. Brown base, blue dress with red dots. Rose shawl with red dots. Baby and woman blonde. (Collection Mr. & Mrs. Robert M. Fortune.)

POKE BONNET, HN 612. Yellow dress with accents of red and black dots. Green shawl and hat with orange, red, yellow and black fan. (Collection Mr. & Mrs. Robert M. Fortune.)

is almost hidden by the balloons that she carries. This early figure was illustrated in the 1940 catalog, but is now out of production. The Old Balloon Seller, HN 1315, a seated figure with a basket and a bunch of balloons, is also an early figure, but it is still produced. The next balloon figure, Old Balloon Seller and Doggy, HN 1791, is mounted on a base with a Doulton puppy. Balloon Man, HN 1954, is a seated figure of a man with balloons. Biddy Penny Farthing, HN 1843, is a standing figure of a woman carrying balloons. The balloon subject has proved so popular that three figures are in current production. Of course the discontinued Balloon Seller, HN 583, long out of production, is the one most sought by collectors.

The figure of the lavender seller was also produced in various different designs. The first Lavender Woman, HN 22, was modeled by Phoebe Stabler. The figure was produced in several colors combined with blues ranging from light to dark. The same figure was given the number HN 342 a few years later after small changes were made in the model. There were also two other figures with similar names; Sweet Lavender, HN 1373, a standing figure, 9 inches high; and a seated figure, Old Lavender Seller, HN 1492, 6¼ inches high. The most valuable figure is the early HN 22. Doulton also produced a seated figure with two children for commercial use for Old English Lavender.

The Pearly Boy, HN 1482, and Pearly Girl, HN 1483, both 5½ inches, are among the most popular figures sought by collectors today. The figures represent children of costermongers of the London markets dressed in festive costumes embroidered with pearl buttons. The figures were illustrated in a catalog of the 1930s with black hats. The Master List describes them as wearing black hats and gives the introduction date as 1931. No date is given for their deletion. They were also produced with red hats, HN 1547 and HN 1548, but no dates of introduction or deletion are given. The Pearly children with the numbers HN 2035 and HN 2036 are illustrated in a catalog and included in a price list of February 1, 1950. There is a later pair of Pearly children with the boy's hands flat against his chest, probably to prevent breakage. In *Collector's Book No. 4*, circa 1952, this version is illustrated with the numbers HN 2035, HN 2036.

The pages of Dickens's writings live in the Royal Doulton figures depicting well-known characters from Dickens's novels. There were several different series of figures modeled by Leslie Harradine and produced at Doulton Lambeth for the Dickens Centenary in 1912. There were six white-glazed and brown stoneware figures including Sam Weller, Mr. Pickwick, Mr. Squeers, Sairey Gamp, Mr. Pecksniff, and Mr. Micawber. The figures were from 6 inches to 9¼ inches high and were set on square bases with the name of the character impressed on the front panel of the base. There was also a set of figures in light brown salt glaze. Leslie Harradine also modeled another set of salt glazed figures set on round bases with supporting bushes and books. Later bone china Dickens figures were made at Burslem. These are similar in design to the stoneware figures and are undoubtedly based on the original Harradine designs. There were three series of six Dickens figures, each, produced at Burslem. The first group includes the figures Pecksniff, Uriah Heep, Fat Boy, Mr. Pickwick, Sairey Gamp, and Mr. Micawber with marks from HN 553 through HN 558. These were produced in the late 1920s and 1930s and were ilustrated in a catalog of the time together with figures from a series of small, 4-inch Dickens figures that were produced from new designs not based on the Harradine figures. The series also included new characters. The figures were on square, undecorated bases and had no HN numbers. By 1940 the series included eighteen figures: Alfred Jingle, Artful Dodger, Bill Sykes, Bumble, Buz Fuz, Captain Cuttle, Fagin, Fat Boy, Little Nell, Micawber, Pecksniff, Pickwick, Sairey Gamp, Sam Weller, Stiggins, Tiny Tim, Tony Weller, and Uriah Heep. More figures were added each year, and by 1950 there were twenty-four of these small figures listed in the catalogs. They were priced at $4. This collection of small Dickens characters is still produced, and the figures were illustrated in January, 1973, *Figure Collector's Book.* In the 1975 catalog of prices, the figures are listed at $12 each. They are made of earthenware.

A later series of large figures includes Mr. Pecksniff, HN 1891; Uriah Heep, HN 1892; Fat Boy, HN 1893; Mr. Pickwick, HN 1894; Mr. Micawber, HN 1895; and Sairey Gamp, HN 1896. A still later series includes numbers HN 2096 through HN 2101. These were made of earthenware in about 1950-1953 and were discontinued in the late 1960s. The most interesting series was that with marks HN 553 through HN 558, not only because of age, but because of detail and coloring. The designs using books and bushes as supports are similar to those designed by Harradine and produced at Lambeth. They also relate to the eighteenth century Staffordshire figures.

Some Royal Doulton figures illustrate styles of dress, for example, Crinoline, Lady in Elizabethan Dress, Lady of the Georgian Period, Pantalettes, Karen in Riding Costume, Poke Bonnet, Regency, Camille, and Girl in Twentieth Century Dress.

There are groups of figures sitting on sofas of Louis XV and Louis XVI style that seem to have drawn inspiration from Sevres groups. These include Tête-a-Tête, Belle-O'-the Ball, Afternoon Tea, Teresa, Fiona, Love Letter, and Repose. In fact there are enough of these group figures to center a collection in this category.

Figures of the dance include Minuet, Gypsy Dance, The Polka, The Lambeth Walk (a figure that was introduced in the late 1930s when the dance was the craze), and The Hornpipe. The group of figures that relates to the ballet is of special interest to collectors. These include Ballet Dancer, Ballerina, Coppelia (from the ballet of that name), La Sulphide, Forest Glade, and Giselle. These are graceful figures with delicate coloring. They were illustrated in color in *Figure Book No. 4.* All are now discontinued.

Collectors are also searching for Art Deco figures since Art Deco is now the craze. These figures were first produced in the late 1930s. Many were re-issued through the years, but all are now discontinued. The figures include Pierrette, Scotties, Angela, Folly, Marietta, The Mask, Butterfly Girl, Sea Sprite, Wood Nymph, and Teenager.

The group of Fairy figures produced in the late 1920s and now discontinued are especially valuable figures. There are seven little 2½- to 3-inch figures of nude fairies sitting among blossoms, and two larger figures, 4 inches, of a fairy sitting on a mushroom. It is not known how many of these figures were produced. Although they were re-issued, they are hard to find. Also, although there is no data in the records, the figures may have been designed by Phoebe Stabler who was known for her sculptures of fairy figures.

Wall masks were a popular item of interior decoration in the 1930s. In c. 1933 Royal Doulton produced a group of masks including Girl with Cap, HN 1590; Girl with Short Bobbed Hair, HN 1593; Girl with Hat, HN 1612; Jester, HN 1611; Baby, HN 1608; and Pompadour, HN 1824. These masks were made in models of pink, blue, or green. Between 1933 and 1939 several decorative masks were modeled by the sculptor, Richard Garbe. These included Lion of the East, HN 1781; Fate, HN 1782; and St. Agnes, HN 1789-1790. The St. Agnes mask was produced in several different colors. These masks by Garbe were produced in editions limited to 100 each, which makes them rare items. Two clown figures, male and female were made as wall vases. They are pale pink, ornamented with gold leaves, and are often found signed, "Noke."

Doulton always catered to the style of the moment and to the demands and tastes of the average public.

MAMSELL, HN 786. "Potted." Pink dress with black trim and design. Black base, shoes, hat. Blonde hair. Nude cupid at base. (Collection Mr. & Mrs. Robert M. Fortune.)

ORANGE VENDER, HN 72, "Potted," c.1926. Light green robe, darker green hooded cape. Brown face, black beard. (Collection Mr. & Mrs. Robert M. Fortune.)

Characters
From Dickens

SAIREY GAMP, HN 2100, L/S. 1953-1967. (Courtesy Doulton & Co., Ltd.)

MR. MICAWBER, HN 2097, L/S. 1953-1967. (Courtesy Doulton & Co., Ltd.)

MR. PECKSNIFF, HN 2098, L/S. 1953-1967. (Courtesy Doulton & Co. Ltd.)

FAT BOY, HN 2096, L/S. 1953-1967. (Courtesy Doulton & Co., Ltd.)

URIAH HEEP, HN 2101, L/S. 1953-1967. Book support at base. (Doulton & Co., Ltd.)

MR. PICKWICK with bush support at base. HN 556 c. 1920-25). (Courtesy Richard Wright.)

MR. PICKWICK, HN 2099, L/S. 1953-1967. (Courtesy Doulton & Co. Ltd.)

To meet the demand of collectors of tiny things, Royal Doulton produced a group of miniature figurines. The figures were 4 inches high and, according to the catalog, "the colourings are different being appropriate to the diminutive size. Miniatures also have their own mark, "M" with a number." There are two catalogs that each devote a page to miniatures; a few illustrations of others are scattered through various other catalogs. The following is a list of figurines that have been found with "M" marks:

Victorian Lady	M 1 & M 11
Paisley Shawl	M 4
Sweet Anne	M 5
Patricia	M 7
Chloe	M 9 & M 10
Little Bridesmaid	M 12
Priscilla	M 14
Pantalettes	M 15 & M 16
Polly Peachum (Curtseying)	M 21
Rosamund	M 33
Denise	M 34 & M 35
Norma	M 36
Erminie	M 40
June	M 65
Janet	M 69 & M 75
Goody Two Shoes	M 80
Bo-Peep	M 82
Maureen	M 84
Robin	M 38

Left to right: DENISE, M 34. Pale green dress, rose overskirt, blue bodice and cap. PAISLEY SHAWL, M. 4. Pale green dress, rose and blue shawl, black bonnet with rose plume. DAINTY MAY, M 73. Rose dress, green underskirt and hat. SWEET ANNE, M 27. Ivory and blue dress, rose jacket and bonnet with blue ribbons. PRISCILLA, M 13. Pale green-blue and yellow dress, green bonnet. PATRICIA, M 7. Skirt pink to lavender, blue jacket, pink hat. POLLY PEACHUM CURTSEYING, M 21. Royal blue and navy dress, white cap. (Collection Mrs. Crayton K. Black.)

BRIDESMAID
M.12

GOODY TWO SHOES
M.80

BO PEEP
M.82

JANET
M.69

PAISLEY SHAWL
M.4

SWEET ANNE
M.5

CHLOE
M.10

POLLY PEACHMAN
M.21

MAUREEN

PANTALETTES

JANET

JUNE

Group of miniatures. Top row, left to right: BRIDESMAID, M 12, rainbow colors. GOODY TWO SHOES, M 80. Red bodice and overskirt, blue skirt. BO-PEEP, M 82. Red bodice and overskirt, pink skirt. JANET, M 69. rainbow colors. Center row, left to right: PAISLEY SHAWL, M 4. Pale green dress, rose and blue shawl. SWEET ANNE, M 5. Blue and ivory dress, red and blue jacket, green bonnet. CHLOE, M 10. Shaded blue skirt, pink hat. POLLY PEACHUM CURTSEYING, M 21. Deep rose costume, white cap. Bottom row, left to right: MAUREEN, M 84, rainbow colors. PANTALETTES, M 15. Pale blues and pink. JANET, M 75. Green overskirt, white underskirt. JUNE, M 65. Lavender, pinks and rose. (Courtesy Doulton & Co. Ltd.)

The majority of these miniature figures was made in the late 1930s; the first list being in the Doulton *Figure Book No. 8.* There were not a great number made. However, since some of the numbers are in the eighties, there may have been as many as 100 different models made in miniature. The popular Sweet and Twenty was made in 3½ inches as well as 6 inches, but for some reason was never given an "M" number. Several miniature figures were made in more than one color and thus have more than one "M" number.

There was also a group of small miniature-sized figures of children dressed in long, fancy dresses. These 4- to 5- inch figures include the early Marie, Daisy, Babie, Rosebud, Rose, Tinkle Bell, Tootles, Dinky Do, Cookie, and Pinkie. In fact these childhood figures proved so popular that they were added to year by year, and there were six pages in color in the *Figure Collector's Book No. 14* issued in January, 1975. There is a little girl with her rag doll, child with a bunny, and child groups such as Bedtime Story, Picnic, and Home Again. The complete list in production includes:

Marie, HN 1370	This Little Pig, HN 1793
Babie, HN 1679	Daydreams, HN 1731
Ivy, HN 1768	Tinkle Belle, HN 1677
Debbie, HN 2385	Home Again, HN 2167
The Bridesmaid, HN 2196	Cissie, HN 1809
Belle, HN 2340	Monica, HN 1467
Peggy, HN 2038	Vanity, HN 2475
Alice, HN 2158	Dinky Do, HN 1678
Picnic, HN 2308	The Rag Doll, HN 2142
Lavinia, HN 1955	Francine, HN 2422
Rose, HN 1368	Bedtime, HN 1978
Valerie, HN 2107	Goody Two Shoes, HN 2037
Wendy, HN 2109	Affection, HN 2236
Penny, HN 2338	Linda, HN 2106
The Bedtime Story, HN 2059	Mary Had a Little Lamb, HN 2048
Cherie, HN 2341	Bo-Peep, HN 1811
Fair Maiden, HN 2211	Darling, HN 1985
Make Believe, HN 2225	Lydia, HN 1908

Although Doulton at one time produced a group of Nursery Rhyme figures, it will be noted that only Bo-Peep, Mary Had a Little Lamb, and This Little Pig remain in production. This makes the other Nursery Rhyme figures, Jack and Jill, Mary, Mary, Wee Willie Winkie, Curly Locks, and the also discontinued Once Upon a Time, He Loves Me, and She Loves Me Not, desirable collectors' pieces.

There is also the group of earlier children's figures made between 1913 and 1920 after the success of the figure Darling. These include: Child and Crab, HN 32; Child Under Cranberry Bush, HN 49; Shy Anne, HN 60 and 64; The Child's Grace, HN 62; The Little Land, HN 63 and 67; and Upon Her Cheeks She Wept, HN 59, HN 511, and HN 522. Then there are the three figures of little nude children listed as Child Studies. The numbers of these figures include HN 1540 through HN 1546 and they are given poetic titles in the Doulton Master List. Many of these early child figures have their titles inscribed on the front of the bases. When first issued the majority of the earliest figures, such as Darling, did not have numbers, but were given HN numbers, later. Although Darling has been produced in several sizes and under many different numbers, the other early child figures have been out of production for a number of years.

In the early 1930s Doulton introduced a series of bone china dishes for children called Bunnykins. These included mugs, plates, oatmeal bowls, and cups and saucers. This nursery china has proved so popular

Left to right: BEDTIME, HN 1978; DINKY DO, HN 1678; DARLING, HN 1985.

through the years that in c. 1973, Doulton introduced a group of Bunny-kin figures. These little figures showed the bunnies dressed as humans, playing and doing housework. The figures include: Billie Bunnykins Cooling Off; Billie and Buntie Bunnykins, Sleigh Ride; Daisie Bunnykins, Springtime; Dollie Bunnykins, Playtime; Bunnykins, Family Photograph; Buntie Bunnykins, Helping Mother; Mr. Bunnykins, Autumn Days; and Mrs. Bunnykins, Clean Sweep. Other figures include Rise and Shine, Story Time, Busy Needles and Tally Ho. These figures are inexpensive and when some are discontinued they are bound to be collectors' pieces.

Children's figures have always been an important item at Royal Doulton, and new children's series continue to be introduced. Within the last few years Doulton has also stepped up their production of birds and domestic animals such as dogs, cats, and horses. In the late 1960s Doulton began producing a group of Beswick figures. These included horses and foals and various breeds of ponies; birds, dogs, cats, cattle, and foxes. There is also a large group of figures from illustrations by Beatrix Potter, a series of figures from the children's book, *Winnie the Pooh,* and a group of figures from *Alice in Wonderland.* New figures in 1976 include four figures, the first in the range of Kate Greenaway children dressed in the quaint costumes of the early nineteenth century. These late figures would be a good field for the beginning collector. In time they will probably be as popular and valuable as the earlier figures. Even today with rising costs of production, their value goes up from year to year.

Discontinued figures of children. Top, left to right: JILL, HN 2061; JACK, HN 2060; LITTLE BOY BLUE, HN 2062. Lower, left to right; LITTLE JACK HORNER, HN 2063; MY PRETTY MAID, HN 2064; JERSEY MILK MAID, HN 2057. (Courtesy Doulton & Co., Ltd.)

Through the years Royal Doulton has produced a number of figures relating to music. These include The Fiddler, The Cellist, Melody, Rhythm, Rhapsody, Symphony, and the limited edition of Women Musicians. This would be an interesting category for the collector, and, coupled with dancing and ballet figures, it would make a sizable group. This group could be enlarged to include the limited edition of eighteenth century lady musicians.

Many Doulton figures were made in earthenware. These include Jester, HN 1702; The Cobbler, HN 1705; Sir Walter Raleigh, HN 1751; The Squire, HN 1814; The Huntsman, HN 1815; Odds and Ends, HN 1844; Orange Vender, HN 1966; Forty Winks, HN 1974. There are others such as the large Parson's Daughter and Margery which were made in earthenware as well as china.

THE HARP, HN 2482. Limited Edition figure (750) by Peggy Davies. Out of production. (Courtesy Doulton & Co.)

THE LUTE, HN 2431, Limited Edition Figure (750) by Peggy Davies. Out of production. (Courtesy Doulton & Co., Ltd.)

Another category of figures includes characters from English country life such as Lambing Time, The Shepherd, Owd Willum, and The Poacher by Harradine. A group of figures that illustrates the Eastern scene is also in general production. The Mendicant could have been lifted from a Bombay street, as could The Snake Charmer, and The Carpet Seller was from the Egyptian scene. The Potter is one of the finest figures Doulton ever made.

Figures of Williamsburg were introduced in 1960. These figures depicted craftsmen and other characters who represented life in eighteenth century Colonial Williamsburg. The figures are 5½ to 7½ inches in height. They include The Silversmith, Wigmaker, Blacksmith of Williamsburg, Royal Governor's Cook, Boy from Williamsburg, Child from Williamsburg, Lady from Williamsburg, Gentleman from Williamsburg, and Hostess of Williamsburg. These figures are still in active production, but prices are going up and when they go out of production they will be collectors' items.

Left: MARGERY, HN 1413. Dark red skirt with lighter red overskirt. Green hat with red and blue flowers, red hair. Height 11 inches. **Right: THE COBBLER, HN 1283.** Black turban with white band, red stripe. Gray coat, green sleeves, red shirt, yellow vest, and red shoes. (Collection Mr. & Mrs. Robert M. Fortune.)

THE MOOR, HN 2082, 17½ inches high. Prestige
Figure (current).

ABDULLAH, HN 2104. (Courtesy Doulton & Co., Ltd.)

CARPET SELLER, HN 1464. (Courtesy Doulton & Co., Ltd.)

BLUE BEARD, HN 2105, 19⅝ inches. Browns and greens, (current).

Although the majority of Royal Doulton figures are small, from 3 to 9 inches, larger figures have been produced. There were the figures of The Bather and Atalanta in off-white salt-glazed stoneware modeled by John Broad and produced in 1912-1914. Broad also designed a few bisque-porcelain figures of costumed women between 1919 and 1921. There were also the salt-glazed figures of soldiers by Leslie Harradine made at Lambeth. Large figures made under Noke's direction at Burslem included the figure of St. George, 16 inches, by F. Thoroughgood; King Charles and The Jester, both modeled by Noke; Sir Walter Raleigh; and Bluebeard.

Princess Badoura, a 21-inch figure of a character from *The Arabian Nights*, seated on a richly ornamented elephant modeled after a design by Harry Tittensor, was produced at Burslem in c. 1928. This figure was included in a group of large figures presented under the title, Prestige Figures, in 1963. Other figures in the group are The Moor, 17½ inches; Jack Point, 17 inches; Matador and Bull, 28 inches; Lion on Rock, 12 inches, by Noke; Leopard on Rock, 9 inches; Tiger on Rock, 12 inches; Fighter Elephant, 12 inches; Fox, 10 3/8 inches; St. George, 16 inches; King Charles, 17 inches, by Noke; and The Old King, 11 inches. Several of these figures were from earlier models.

ST. GEORGE, HN 2067. Height 16 inches. Prestige Figure in current production. (Courtesy Doulton & Co., Ltd.)

Left: **PARSON'S DAUGHTER, HN 338.** Red shawl
and hat, yellow dress with green, brown, and blue
patches on skirt. Right: **VICTORIAN LADY, HN
728,c.1936.** Dress shaded from pink to white, purple
hat with blue feather, shawl shaded from pink to
purple. (Collection Mr. & Mrs. Robert M. Fortune.)

Certain Royal Doulton figures have a special interest for the advanced
collector. These include such figures as those by the artists Phoebe
Stabler, Charles Vyse, Charles J. Noke, Leslie Harradine and the sculptor
Richard Garbe. Some of these figures such as those by Richard Garbe
were produced in limited editions and most of them are no longer in
production. Of course, when a figure has been reproduced, the one
with the low production number is the oldest and most valuable.

Records of the Doulton Company concerning the production of
figurines are incomplete and often confusing. Sometimes the exact date
when a figure was produced is not known because it was not recorded or
has been lost. Also, the date of withdrawal, or when a figure was discontinued, is not always recorded. Thus, the collector must beware not to
buy a figure represented as old which is really a production of a later date.
For example, the Victorian Lady is an early figure. The first production
number of this figurine was HN 728, and it was produced between 1925
and 1928. Because of its popularity it was re-issued through the years
under various numbers.

Numbers of figures were changed when there were modifications in
size, color, or detail in the design of the figure. Some of the early figures
such as the Forty Thieves series have been re-issued under thirty different

Two of **FORTY THIEVES. Left:** Green coat and orange turban. **Right:** Brown pants, orange coat, brown, orange, and green turban. Early figures with no HN number. (Collection Mr. & Mrs. Robert M. Fortune.)

numbers and Jester and Darling have many different production numbers. Several figures have modifications in design because of breakage. For example The Carpet Seller which was first introduced in January, 1931, has been found with the impressed date, 2-11-31. The model has extended fingers on the right hand, while subsequent models have the fingers wrapped around the carpet to avoid breakage. A similar situation happened with a more recent figurine, Gypsy Dance, which was first introduced in 1955 with arm extended and fingers open. This model was discontinued December 31, 1956, because of the high percentage of loss in production due to the fingers being broken. The figure was re-introduced January 1, 1959, with the hand on the extended arm holding the skirt. This second model was deleted December 31, 1970. When a figure is resculptured to correct a problem such as that of the finger, the modeler sometimes reduces his model in size. There are also differences in size between the same models made in earthenware and in bone china. When Doulton went out of the earthenware business in 1960, the earthenware figures were made in china in the same molds that had been used for earthenware figures. Since a china body shrinks more in firing than an earthenware body, the china figure would be smaller. For example: the earthenware Sir Walter Raleigh, HN 1751, is 11½ inches, and the china figure, HN 1742, is slightly smaller. The figures Biddy and Rita are an

30

Left: PRISCILLA, HN 1340, "Potted." Deep pink ruffled dress with blue bonnet and parasol, white pantalettes and red shoes. Right: RITA, HN 1448. "Potted" and dated 1933, 7¼ inches. Rose shaded to pink dress; green shawl with red and yellow flowers. (Collection Mr. & Mrs. Robert M. Fortune.)

example of two sizes of a figure given a different name. Both figures have the same registry number, but different names and different HN numbers. Biddy, HN 1445, is 5 inches tall. The figure was also made in orange, HN 1500, and red, HN 1513. Rita, HN 1448, is red, "potted" and dated 1933. The figure is 7¼ inches tall. Rita, HN 1450, is blue. This is only one instance of the confusion that makes it difficult to give exact information about many of the figures.

Royal Doulton figures are usually made in a choice of colors. Pink, green, and red are favorite colors, and figures such as Autumn Breezes and Top-of-the-Hill are made in all of these colors. Other figures are produced in multicolor rainbow colors and there are also figures produced with gray or mauve predominating, while some figures are a combination of blue and green, pink and blue, red and yellow, or blue and brown. The Orange Lady was produced with a Paisley shawl, HN 1759, and later with a green shawl, HN 1953. A small number of figures were produced in plain ivory, and a few figures were made in black and yellow.

There are also figures with dresses ornamented with dots, flowers and, sometimes, with accents of gilt as in Gentleman in Period Dress, HN 635, and Lady in Period Dress, HN 637.

China flowers made in naturalistic forms are a specialty of Royal

31

Left: JANICE, HN 2022 (green). Right:
ORANGE LADY, HN 1953 (green skirt.)
(Courtesy Doulton & Co., Ltd.)

Left: HINGED PARASOL, HN 1578. Green parasol
and hat; dress, rose shading to green with blue dots.
Right: CHLOE, HN 1470, "Potted." Dress rainbow
colors, green, yellow, rose. Hat orchid, blue, and
rose; bouquet blue and rose. (Collection Mr. & Mrs.
Robert M. Fortune.)

Doulton, and in addition to the pots and baskets of flowers sold separately, flowers are used to add decorative notes to many figurines. Little girls carry nosegays or baskets of flowers, and such figures as Daffy-down Dilly, Springflowers, Lydia, and Janet carry flowers. In The Flowerseller's Children, Granny's Heritage, Curly Nob, and Bonnie Lassie, flowers form a dominant part of the composition. Hats, muffs, shawls, fans, and parasols are also used to add to the decorative effects of many of the figures.

Figures in different colors are given different numbers, and a different number is given for each color. The early figure Crinoline was made in mauve, green with lithographed flowers, and green without flowers. Each variation was given a different number. When one of the variations of a figure is discontinued that becomes the most important number of the figure.

Some figures were also made in several sizes. Paisley Shawl, HN 1987, is large-sized, and HN 1988 is medium-sized. Also the popular Sweet and Twenty is made in 6 inch and in 3½ inch sizes. Then there is the group of figures made in miniature size as well as regular size.

Marks on Royal Doulton figures are often confusing. Some of the early figures were hand-lettered "Potted by Doulton" instead of the trademark, but even though the current trademark was adopted in 1902, many figurines such as Puff and Powder, HN 433, 1924, were still hand-lettered, "Potted by Doulton." A reliable source at the Doulton factory states that the practice of hand-lettering the wording "Potted by Doulton" continued until the start of World War II. The wording was applied by the particular artist responsible for decorating the figure. Over the years three

Left: ERMINE COAT, HN 1981 (red dress). Center: SUSAN, HN 2056 (blue). Right: SUZETTE, HN 1487 (pink).

different colors were used — red, olive green, and black. There was strict control over the style of lettering which had to be used; however, the style seems to have varied. Some figures such as Puff and Powder, HN 433, are marked in old English, and Tête-a-Tête, HN 798, also an early figure, is marked in script. The early Balloon Seller is marked with the date, 3/11/1936, and, also, "Potted by Doulton" in ornate lettering that covers almost the whole base. The early St. George, HN 385, is marked "Potted by Doulton," and the later figure is also marked "Potted." If a careful study of the individual artists who painted the figures were possible, much new information about the "Potted" mark might come to light.

The following figures have recently been found with the hand-lettered mark "Potted by Doulton":

Angela, HN 1206
Anthea, HN 1527
Balloon Seller, HN 583
Bonnie Lassie, HN 1626
Bride, HN 1600
Chloe, HN 1450;1470
Cerise, HN 1607
Curley Nob, HN 1627
Doris Keane, HN 90
Estelle, HN 1566
Georgian Lady, HN 41
Greta, HN 1485
Granny's Shawl, HN 1647
Hinged Umbrella, HN 1548
Lady Fayre, HN 1265
Little Bridesmaid, HN 1433
London Cry, HN 452
Darling, HN 1319.3/11/39
Mamsell, HN 786
Mermaid, HN 97
Monica, HN 1467; HN 1456
Marietta, HN 1341
Marie, HN 1416
Miss Demure, HN 1402
Orange Seller, HN 1325
Orange Vender, HN 72
Paisley Shawl, HN 1460
Pantalettes, HN 1862
Patricia, HN 1414
Pied Piper, HN 1215
Polly Peachum, HN 549
Pamela, HN 1468
Puff and Powder, HN 433
Phyllis, HN 1456
Priscilla, HN 1337; HN 1340; 1360
Rita, HN 1448
Sairey Gamp, HN 558
Scotties, HN 1281
Spook, HN 50 (Tittensor)
St. George, HN 385
Suzette, HN 1487
Sweet & Twenty, HN 1298; 1589; 1360
Sweet Anne, HN 1318; HN 1496
Tête-a-Tête, HN 798
Shy Anne, HN 64
The Bather, HN 687
Victorian Lady, HN 727; HN 1276

The above list is far from complete, and it should be noted that some

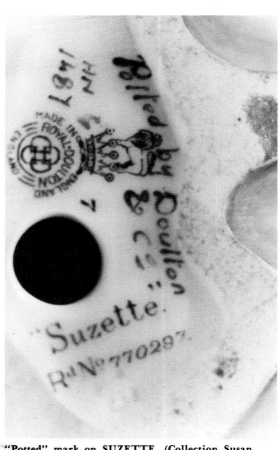

"Potted" mark on SUZETTE. (Collection Susan Kasulka.)

Three small girls. Left: CERISE, HN 1607. Pale pink dress with blue flowers, blue hat with red bow, brown basket with reddish purple cherries. Center: LUCY ANN, HN 1502. Pink dress with blue shading, blue ribbons and shoes. Holding red, blue, and white flowers in skirt. Right: GRETA, HN 1485. Dress and shawl in shades of pink, white pantalettes. Basket with red and blue flowers. (Collection Mr. & Mrs. Robert M. Fortune.)

models of a figure were marked "Potted" and others were not. Also many figures were dated and some were both dated and "Potted." For example, The Parson's Daughter, HN 564, is "Potted" and dated 1/11/27.

The usual mark for Royal Doulton figures is the design number preceded by the letters HN plus the Doulton trademark, the name of the figure, and sometimes the artist's name such as Noke or Harradine. The trademark, in addition to the number, helps establish the year of production. The following chart indicates, approximately, the periods when figures were introduced:

Figure Book No. 1
        HN I-80 . . . . June 1913 onwards
Figure Book No. 2
        HN 82-359 . . . . No dates
Figure Book No. 3
        HN 361-456 . . . . No dates
Figure Book No. 4
        HN 459-714 . . . . No dates
Figure Book No. 5
        HN 715-1402 . . . . 1925 onwards

Left: BRIDE, HN 1600, "Potted," c.1934. White dress with pink shading, yellow roses. Right: ESTELLE, HN 1566, "Potted." White dress shaded from blue to pink, blue shoes, muff and hat. (Collection Mr. & Mrs. Robert M. Fortune.)

Figure Book No. 6
        HN 1403-1656 . . . . 1930 onwards
Figure Book No. 7
        HN 1657-1865 . . . . No dates
Figure Book No. 8
        HN 1866-2327 . . . . 1938 — present - day
        HN 2038 1941
        HN 2058 1947
        HN 2079,2042/43/45/2050 1948
        HN 2085-8 1950
        HN 2107/8;2114/17 1951
        HN 2147/8;2150 1955
        HN 2149 1957
        HN 2133 1958
        HN 2128,2116,2151 1961
        HN 2184,2132 1962
        HN 2255, 2306, 2152 1964
        HN 2311, 2327, 2271 1965
        HN 2362-2398 1970

The above chart was released by Doulton & Co. several years ago. Although it is not entirely dependable, it can serve as a rough guide. The Master List which accompanies the above chart gives complete individual listings of production and withdrawal dates, but I have not included it here because, again, there are mistakes which can only be corrected with a complete checking of all figures including the trial pieces as well as the models actually produced.

Left: LONDON CRY, HN 452, "Potted." Boy in green jacket and hat, white blouse, holding orange carrots and onions. Woman with purple skirt, red blouse, white apron and hat. Basket with carrots and greens. **Right: TWO A PENNY, HN 1359.** Figure in green skirt, maroon blouse, cream apron, yellow scarf, green stripes, green hat feather. Red, green, and yellow articles on tray. (Collection Mr. & Mrs. Robert M. Fortune.)

Instead I have compiled my own list which gives all the HN numbers, but does not give introduction or withdrawal dates.

The question of the number of pieces of each figure which was produced is also unanswered. First of all there were limited editions of certain figures such as the masks and figurines produced from designs by the sculptor Richard Garbe. These were in editions of 50 and 100. Compare this to the present-day editions of 1,000 to 15,000 pieces in limited editions of plates.

The general production issues of early figurines was small, since the molds were made of plaster of paris which was capable of producing only a small number of models (about three dozen) before the mold detail was no longer clear or sharp and a new mold had to be made. How many times the mold was renewed depended upon the demand for the figure. When a mold was renewed, any mistakes or imperfections were usually corrected, and this explains the occasional differences in models. Today, because of the use of plastic molds, the number of models made in a particular mold is almost unlimited, and thousands of each figure are produced. Again, the demand of the public controls the number of each figure produced, and unpopular figures are withdrawn and not repeated if they have not sold well.

Although all figures are carefully inspected before leaving the factory, some figures are better modeled and some are more expertly painted due to the skill of the particular painter. Also the coloring often varies, and some figures have clearer, brighter color. The discriminating collector will inspect each figure carefully before buying, for perfection of detail of modeling and of color.

STATUETTES
Royal Doulton Bone China

Page from Doulton catalog, c. 1930.

In their advertising Doulton always stressed the use of figurines in
interior decoration. Early catalogs give notes about the placing of figurines in a room. "One or two Royal Doulton figures suffice in themselves
to strike the colour keynote of a room. For the center of a mantlepiece,
for example, could anything be more charming than a group of two Royal
Doulton Chelsea figures before an old mirror, flanked at each side by
candlesticks festooned with pear-shaped crystals? Or on the side table
reserved for the smoking things and the book or two one is reading, what
more enticing than an electric lamp made up of Royal Doulton statuettes?"
A note in another catalog reads: "A Doulton figure in suitable colours
makes a beautiful center for the tea table and is as decorative to any room
as a vase of flowers." And again: "The use of Doulton figures and lamps
as table decorations during meals is already a fashion with people of
exclusive tastes." A Doulton catalog of the 1930s illustrates a page of

ROYAL DOULTON ELECTRIC LAMPS
IN MANY STYLES AND COLOURS

"Veronica" (18 in.).
L 11517.

"Cerise" (13 in.).
L 21607.

"Fleurette" (15 in.).
L 31587.

"Clotilde" (19 in.).
L 41599.

MODERN DECORATIVE LAMPS
OF ROYAL DOULTON

"Janet" (14½ in.).
L 17.

"Irene" (17 in.).
L 81621.

"Rose" (14 in.).
L 30.

The Hinged Parasol (14 in.).
L 51578.

Further details of Lamps on inside of back cover.

Group of lamps with figures. (Page taken from Doulton catalog of mid-1930s.)

electric lamps with Doulton figures set on mahogany or alabaster bases and various shapes of harmonizing shades. The figures for the lamps were given special numbers. For example: Sweet and Twenty mounted as a lamp is L8 1710 (pink); Aileen has the lamp number LX 1664; Clemency (green) has the number LX 1634; while the 10-inch Parson's Daughter is HN 564 mounted as a lamp. The catalog states: "All the figures shown in the brochure may be obtained mounted as electric lamps. These were probably sent to a special mounting company, as were the lamps made of Worcester china figures at this time. Royal Doulton figures were also mounted on ashtrays, and miniature figures were mounted on marble or mahogany bookends. Some figures have been found with small holes in their bases indicating that they have been mounted either on lamp bases or bookends. Small Dickens figures were set on napkin rings.

Royal Doulton figures appealed to the taste of the early twentieth

VICTORIAN LADY

M R. PICKWICK

BUTTERFLY GIRL

Royal Doulton figures sporting their various charms beneath a gay canopy of colour, introduces a new note in modern electric lighting and decoration. THE CHELSEA PAIR are the figures used for this Lamp.

POLLY PEACHUM

PIERRETTE

BALLOONS

TÊTE-À-TÊTE

PARSON'S DAUGHTER

[10]

A Vogue which has come to stay

IN THE OLD Victorian days, the ornaments in massed formation had perforce to play a secondary part to the heavy furniture and draperies of the period. In modern *décors*, the fewer pieces of decorative ware, whether of pottery, metal or glass, are given the space to express their several individual characteristics.

One or two Royal Doulton figures suffice in themselves to strike the colour keynote of a room. For the centre of a mantelpiece, for example, could anything be more charming than a group of two Royal Doulton "Chelsea" figures before an old mirror, flanked perhaps at each side by candlesticks festooned with pear-shaped crystals? Or on the side table reserved for the smoking things and the book ✚ or two one is reading, what more enticing than an electric lamp made up of Royal Doulton statuettes?

These figures admirably emphasize the rare quality of Royal Doulton *Fine* China, of which they are made. It is this quality which imbues the colours of these figures with incomparable beauty.

Many well-known artists have designed statuettes for Royal Doulton. Besides those illustrated on the opposite page, one will recognize others like THE LIDO LADY, LADY JESTER, SUZANNAH, CASSIM, BABA, GEISHA and NEGLIGÉE ; also characters from Dickens and "The Beggar's Opera."

Royal Doulton Figures are obtainable at the principal Stores and Royal Doulton Agencies (The Best China Shops), also ✚ *at many leading Goldsmiths.*

[11]

Page from Doulton catalog, 1920s-1930s, featuring Chelsea Pair lamp with ornate silk shade, figurines, and suggestions of how to use them decoratively in the home.

century public when they were first introduced and they have continued to be popular, not only to the person who buys one figure, but to the collector. Indeed, there is a large group of collectors of new as well as discontinued figures. Some collectors buy all colors of a figure and all variations of a model.

Specializing not only increases the value of a collection, but the harder a piece is to find, the more interesting the search. A collection of

PHYLLIS, HN 1456. "Potted."

PATRICIA, HN 1414. "Potted." C. 1930.

LADY FAYRE, HN 1265. "Potted."

LADY ANN NEVILLE, HN 2006. 1948.

BALLOON SELLER, HN 583.

PROMENADE, HN 2076.

42

THE POTTER, HN 1493. Model by Noke.

Two different colors of SWEET ANNE (l) HN, 1496;
(r) HN, 1318. Green and blue, "Potted." (Collection
Susan Kasulka.)

THE FOUR SEASONS. Left to right: SPRING,
HN 2085; SUMMER, HN 2086; AUTUMN, HN
2087; WINTER, HN 2088 c.1951. (Collection Susan
Kasulka.)

Left, MEMORIES, HN 2030.
Right, GOSSIPS, HN 2025.
(Collection Susan Kasulka.)

Left, FARMER'S WIFE, HN 2065.
Center, APPLE MAID, HN 2160.
Right, FRENCH PEASANT, HN 2075.
(Collection Susan Kasulka.)

Left, NOELLE, HN 2179.
Right, CHRISTMAS TIME, HN 2110.
(Collection Susan Kasulka.)

Left, JANICE, HN 2165. Right, HARLEQUIN—
ADE, HN 585. (Collection Susan Kasulka.)

Left, A COURTING, HN 2004 c.1946.Right,
WILLY WON'T HE, HN 2150 c.1954. (Collection
Susan Kasulka.)

GEORGIANA, HN 2093.
(Collection Susan Kasulka.)

LEISURE HOUR, HN 2055 c.1949.
(Collection Susan Kasulka.)

Left, SABBATH MORN, HN 1982 c.1945. Center
THE SKATER, HN 2117. Right, ROSEMARY, HN
2091. (Collection Susan Kasulka.)

Left, DAFFY DOWN DILLY, HN 1712. Center,
BONNIE LASSIE, HN 1626. Right, SPRING
FLOWERS, HN 1807. (Collection Susan Kasulka.)

Group of child figures. Top, SEA SHORE, HN 2283; ONE THAT GOT AWAY, HN 2153; RIVER BOY, HN 2128. Left, BABY BUNTING, HN 2108; right, STAYED AT HOME, HN 2207. Bottom, MY TEDDY, HN 2177; GOLLIWOG, HN 2040; MOTHER'S HELPER, HN 2151; BUNNY, HN 2214; GOLDEN DAYS, HN 2274. (Collection Susan Kasulka.)

Left, ESMERALDA, HN 2168. Center, SCOTTIES, HN 1281, rare. Right, THE BATHER, HN 687, early figure. (Collection Susan Kasulka.)

Left, SWEET AND TWENTY, HN 1298. Center,
SPRING MORNING, HN 1972. Right, TÊTE-A-
TÊTE, HN 499, early and rare.

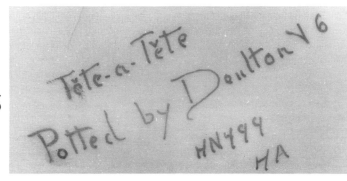

Potted mark on base of figure.
(Collection Susan Kasulka.)

MARIETTA, HN 1341.
(Collection Susan Kasulka.)

Right, FLEURETTE with fan. HN 1587. Left:
MISS WINSOME, HN 1665.

Royal Doulton figures can center on subjects such as historical characters which would include Sir Walter Raleigh; the kings — Henry VII, Henry VIII (limited edition of 200), and King Charles; Period Figures in English History, men and women in period dress; and other period figures. One could specialize in figures of children of which there are many, or one can collect only dogs or other animals. An interesting collection could include only "Potted" figures or signed figures such as those marked Noke, Harradine, or Garbe. Then there are also the interesting Beggar's Opera series, Ali Baba and the Forty Thieves series, or the important Dickens characters.

For the collector of Noke signed pieces there are the following rare and valuable pieces: Doris Keane as Cavallini, HN 90; Cardinal Wolsey, 13½ inches, 1894; Double Jester, made for the Chicago Fair in 1893; The Cobbler, HN 542; Moorish Minstrel, HN 34; The Dunce, HN 6, and Georgian Lady, 11½ inches, "Potted" and signed C.J. Noke, Sc.

According to their custom, Doulton adds new figures each year. The figures are divided between the range of Lovely Ladies and popular character storytelling figures.

New figures added in 1973 include Vanity, HN 2475; At Ease, HN 2473; Victoria, HN 2471; Masque, HN 2554; Lunchtime, HN 2585; and Past Glory, HN 2484; popular figures and a series of new matt finish figures including Dreamweaver, HN 2283; The Judge, HN 2443; Thanksgiving, HN 2446; The Parisian, HN 2445; Bon Appetit, HN 2444; and Seafarer, HN 2455.

Additions to the range of Royal Doulton Lovely Lady figures in 1974 included: Laurianne, HN 2719; Veneta, HN 2772; Fiona, HN 2694; Lady Pamela, HN 2718. The character figures included Old Meg, HN 2494; The Huntsman, HN 2492; The Helmsman, HN 2499; and Good Morning, HN 2671.

The following Lovely Ladies figures were added in 1975: Clarinda, HN 2724; Julia, HN 2705; Grand Manner, HN 2728; Regal Lady, HN 2709; Young Love, HN 2735; Pensive Moments, HN 2704; and Sweet Seventeen, HN 2734. The character figures included Thanks Doc, HN 2731; Taking Things Easy, HN 2677. Country Lass, HN 2099, and The Milkmaid, HN 2100, were old figures re-introduced.

Other figures added to the range of Lovely Ladies in 1974 was the series called Haute Ensemble. These stylized modern figures were about 12 inches in height. They were produced in a matt finish which gives delicate skin tones and a deep gloss to the materials of the dresses. The figures, each the personal creation of an individual artist, included:

Mantilla.	HN 2712
Eliza.	HN 2543
Boudoir	HN 2542
A La Mode	HN 2544
Carmen	HN 2545

In July, 1970, Doulton produced the first two figures of a limited series of eighteenth century lady musicians modeled by the artist Peggy Davies, one of the best known porcelain sculptors in England. The series is comprised of twelve figures of a women's orchestra, each member shown playing an instrument of that era. Each figure was limited to an edition of 750 each. Each piece is signed on the base by the artist Peggy Davies and sequentially numbered. The figures are exquisitely gowned in period costumes, perfectly modeled and hand-painted, and the instruments are meticulously reproduced. The list of the figures with year of introduction and introductory price is as follows:

1970	Cello	$250
	Virginals	250
1972	Lute	250
	Violin	250

TONY WELLER, HN 684. Green coat, mustard inner coat, black hat, red scarf with black dots. (Collection Mr. & Mrs. Robert M. Fortune.)

ELLEN TERRY AS CATHERINE of ARAGON. Doulton Burslem, England mark, inscribed Noke signature, 1894. Height, 12½ inches. (Collection Susan Kasulka.)

49

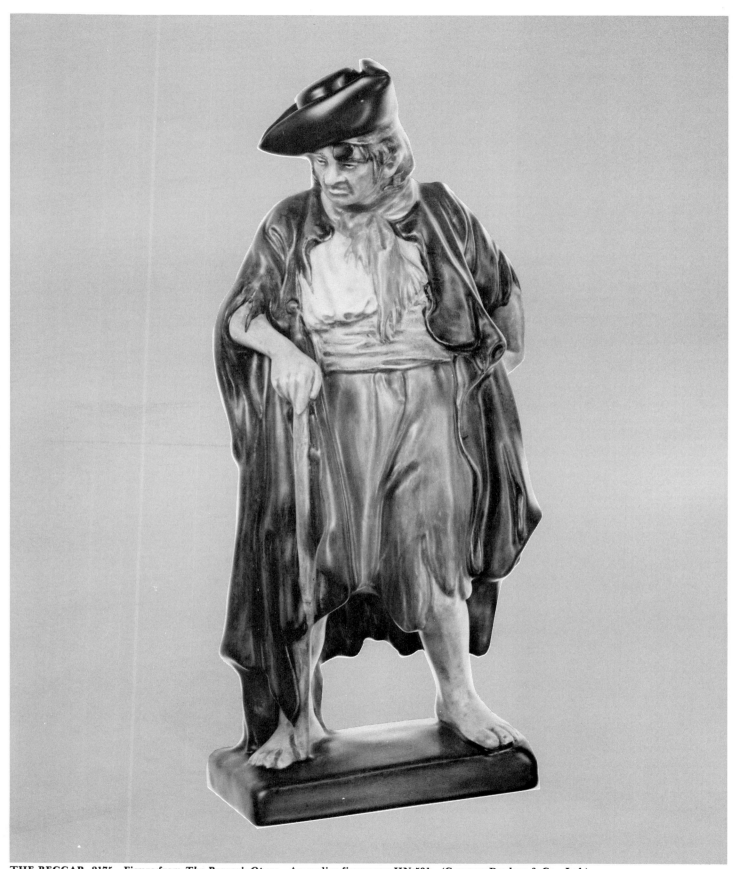

THE BEGGAR, 2175. Figure from *The Beggar's Opera.* An earlier figure was HN 591. (Courtesy Doulton & Co., Ltd.)

1973	Harp	275
	Flute	275
1974	Chitarrone	325
	Cymbals	325
1975	Dulcimer	375
	Hurdy Gurdy	375
1976	French Horn	400
	Viola d'Amore	400

The Lady Musician series of limited-edition figurines is now complete and out of production, and no new models will be added. The figurines are completely sold out except for six pairs of the French Horn and Viola d'Amore. The figures have already increased in value, and prices promise to go much higher.

This is true of all Royal Doulton figures, so whatever category the collector chooses, they are a good investment. The new figures are not only of high quality technically, but the majority of the designs have the aesthetic values of the old figures. Such figures as Victoria and Antoinette have all the charm and grace of the old favorites such as Autumn Breezes and Top O' the Hill. Ascot and Julia are charming Edwardian pieces while Daphne and Lorna have the stylized elongated lines of modern art.

However, some of the newer figures such as the current small Dickens figures, the new matt bisque figures Dreamweaver, Bon Appetit, and Seafarer are close to caricatures. Others, such as A Stitch in Time, Thanks Doc, and Good Morning tell stories that should be left to graphic illustration or to printed matter. These figures were undoubtedly shaped to the taste of the public, but it seems regrettable that the commercial factor should determine the product rather than the artistic tastes of the designers. Since writing the above the writer has received information that some of these figures have been put on the inactive list. Also, the matt series, except for The Judge, has been discontinued. The Judge will now be made with glossy finish. Of course this makes these figures more valuable to the collector.

The complete list of figures discontinued in 1977 include:

HN 2152 Adrienne
HN 2106 Linda
HN 2144 Jovial Monk
HN 2149 Love Letter
HN 2166 Bride
HN 2196 Bridesmaid
HN 2257 Sea Harvest
HN 2256 Twilight
HN 2269 Leading Lady
HN 2347 Nina
HN 2362 Wayfarer
HN 2398 Alexandre
HN 2348 Geraldine

HN 2118 Good King Wenceslas
HN 2102 Pied Piper
HN 2119 Town Crier
HN 2283 Dreamweaver
HN 2375 Viking
HN 2444 Bon Appetit
HN 2446 Thanksgiving
HN 2455 Seafarer
HN 2487 Beachcomber
HN 2491 Old Meg
HN 2546 Buddies
HN 2671 Good Morning
HN 1911 Autumn Breezes

New figures added to the line in 1977 include:

HN 2359 The Detective
HN 2683 Stop Press
HN 2803 First Dance
HN 2807 Stephanie
HN 2810 Solitude
HN 2814 Evening

There are also two new Kate Greenaway figurines, Sophie and Emma.

Many other new projects are being planned by Doulton & Co. for the next year or two, and the collector should watch for the announcement of these. Indeed, one difficulty in writing about products of a company

THE BRIDE, HN 2166. Pink shadings with blue fringe around bouquet. Figure current. (Doulton & Company, Ltd.)

CHARLEY'S AUNT, HN 35. (Collection Ron Heberlee.)

MOORISH MINSTREL, 13 inches high. Burslem mark and inscribed Noke signature. 1897. (Collection Susan Kasulka.)

that is still in existence and production is that the picture changes from year to year as new articles are produced and old ones discontinued. For this reason no book or article can be definitive.

The following is a list of figurines produced between 1913, when the first HN number was assigned, to 1970. The list includes the number of the figure when first produced, the color, and the artist-designer or modeler, when known. The later production numbers within the designated period are also listed. Although the information given is not infallible, it does provide a guide for placing the approximate date when a figure was first produced. The number of repeat productions will assist in determining the rarity of a figure.

Chronological List of Royal Doulton Figures,
1913 - 1970

DARLING. Modeler, Charles Vyse
    HN 1 (large)
    HN 1319 (7½ inches)
    HN 1985 (5¼ inches)
ELIZABETH FRY. Modeler, Charles Vyse
    HN 2
MILKING TIME. Modeler, Phoebe Stabler
    HN 3
    HN 306
PICARDY PEASANT. Modeler, Phoebe Stabler
    HN 4 (blue, female)
    HN 5 (gray, female)
    HN 13 (blue, male)
    HN 17 (blue and green, male)
    HN 19 (green, male)
DUNCE. Modeler, Noke
    HN 6
    HN 357
PEDLAR - WOLF
    HN 7
THE CRINOLINE. Designer, George Lambert
    HN 8 (mauve)
    HN 9 (green, litho. flowers)
    HN 9A (green, no flowers)
    HN 21 (different flowers)
    HN 21A
    HN 650-655

MADONNA OF THE SQUARE. Modeler, Phoebe Stabler
    HN 10 (mauve)
    HN 10A(dark blue)
    HN 11 (gray)
    HN 14 (dark blue)
    HN 27 (green)
    HN 1968 (green)
    HN 1969 (blue)
    HN 2034
BABY
    HN 12

PUSSY
 HN 18
 HN 325
COQUETTE. Designer, William White
 HN 20
 HN 37 (decorated dress)
THE LAVENDER WOMAN. Modeler,
Phoebe Stabler
 HN 22 (light blue)
 HN 23 (darker blue)
 HN 23A (dark blue)
 HN 342
 HN 569
SLEEP
 HN 24 (dove gray)
 HN 25 (blue-green)
 HN 25A (blue-green)
 HN 424
THE SLEEPY SCHOLAR. Modeler,
William White
 HN 15 (blue)
 HN 16 (light green)
 HN 29
THE DILIGENT SCHOLAR. Modeler,
William White
 HN 26
MOTHERHOOD. Modeler, Leslie
Harradine
 HN 28 (light blue)
 HN 30 (patterned dress)
 HN 303
RETURN OF PERSEPHONE. Modeler,
Charles Vyse
 HN 31
CHILD AND CRAB
 HN 32
ARAB FIGURE
 HN 33
 HN 343
MOORISH MINSTREL. Modeler, Noke
 HN 34
 HN 364
 HN 415
 HN 797
CHARLEY'S AUNT
 HN 35
 HN 1554
 HN 1703
THE SENTIMENTAL PIERROT
 HN 36
THE CARPET VENDOR
 HN 38
 HN 76
 HN 348
 HN 350
THE WELSH GIRL
 HN 39

HN 92 (ivory)
 HN 514
 HN 516
 HN 519
 HN 520
 HN 660
 HN 668
 HN 669
 HN 701
 HN 792
LADY OF THE ELIZABETHAN PERIOD
 HN 40
 HN 73 (blue and green)
A LADY OF THE GEORGIAN PERIOD.
Design by E.W. Light
 HN 41
ROBERT BURNS
 HN 42
A WOMAN OF THE TIME OF HENRY VI
 HN 43
A LILAC SHAWL
 HN 44
 HN 362
 HN 442
JESTER. Modeled by Noke
 HN 45 (black and white)
 HN 45A (green and white)
 HN 45B (red and white)
 HN 55
 HN 71
 HN 307
 HN 308
 HN 320
 HN 367
 HN 412
 HN 426
 HN 442
 HN 446
 HN 552
 HN 610
 HN 616
 HN 627
 HN 630
 HN 1295
 HN 1333
 HN 1702
 HN 2016
GAINSBORO HAT
 HN 46 (blue)
 HN 46A (black pattern)
 HN 47 (green)
 HN 329
 HN 383
 HN 675
 HN 705
 HN 453
LADY WITH FAN. Modeled by Richard Garbe
 HN 48 (blue)

HN 52 (green)
HN 53 (blue)
HN 53A (green)
HN 335
HN 509
LADY WITH ROSE. Modeled by Richard
Garbe
   HN 48A
   HN 68
   HN 304
   HN 336
   HN 515
   HN 517
CHILD RESTING UNDER
GOOSEBERRY BUSH
   HN 49
A SPOOK. Modeler, Tittensor
   HN 50 (green)
   HN 51 (red cap)
   HN 58 (red cap)
   HN 512
   HN 1218
THE ERMINE MUFF
   HN 54
   HN 86
   HN 332
   HN 443
   HN 671
THE LANDS OF NOD
   HN 56 (ivory)
   HN 56A (gray)
THE CURTSEY
   HN 57(orange)
   HN 57A (mauve)
   HN 57B
   HN 66A
   HN 334 (mauve & brown)
   HN 327
   HN 363
   HN 371
   HN 518
   HN 547
   HN 629
   HN 670
UPON HER CHEEKS SHE WEPT
   HN 59
   HN 511
   HN 552
SHY ANNE
   HN 60 (light blue, decoration)
   HN 65 (blue with white dots)
   HN 64 (ivory)
   HN 568
KATHARINE(KATHERINE)
   HN 61
   HN 74
   HN 341

HN 471
A CHILD'S GRACE
   HN 62
THE LITTLE LAND
   HN 63 (green)
   HN 67 (mauve)
THE FLOUNCED SKIRT
   HN 66
   HN 77 (yellow)
   HN 78 (white with decoration)
PRETTY LADY
   HN 69 (blue)
   HN 70 (gray)
   HN 302
   HN 330
   HN 361
   HN 384
   HN 565
   HN 763
ORANGE VENDER
   HN 72
   HN 508
   HN 521
BLUEBEARD
   HN 75
   HN 410
   HN 2105
SHYLOCK
   HN 79
   HN 317
WAITING FOR THE BOATS
   HN 80
   HN 631
SHEPHERD. Modeled by Harradine
   HN 81
   HN 617
   HN 632
   HN 1975
SHEPHERDESS
   HN 735
THE AFTERNOON CALL
   HN 82
THE LADY ANNE
   HN 83 (yellow)
   HN 87 (green)
   HN 93 (blue)
MANDARIN
   HN 84
   HN 316
   HN 318
   HN 366
   HN 382
   HN 450
   HN 460 (green)
   HN 461 (red)
   HN 601
   HN 602
   HN 611

HN 746
HN 787
HN 791
JACK POINT. Noke
  HN 85
  HN 91 (black checks)
  HN 99
  HN 2080 (L/S)
DOUBLE SPOOK
  HN 88 (green caps)
  HN 89 (red caps)
  HN 372
DORIS KEANE AS CAVALLINI.
Noke model
  HN 90
  HN 96
  HN 345
  HN 467
THE YOUNG KNIGHT
  HN 94
EUROPA
  HN 95
MERMAID
  HN 97
  HN 300
GUY FAWKES
  HN 98
  HN 347
  HN 445
PIPER NIGGER MINSTREL
  HN 301
  HN 328
  HN 416
SCRIBE
  HN 305
  HN 324
  HN 1235
FIGURED CRINOLINES
  HN 309
DUNCE'S CAP
  HN 310
DANCING FIGURE
  HN 311
SPRING
  HN 312
  HN 472
  HN 1774
  HN 2085
SUMMER
  HN 313
  HN 473
  HN 2086
AUTUMN
  HN 314
  HN 474
  HN 2087
WINTER
  HN 315

Top, left to right: PEARLY BOY, HN 1482 (black hat, hands out); SONIA, HN 1692 (pink hat and blouse, skirt tinged with pink and yellow. Cushion on seat green-blue. PEARLY GIRL, HN 1483 (black hat). Lower left; DARBY, HN 1427. Right: JOAN, HN 1422. (Courtesy Doulton & Co., Ltd.)

THE SHEPHERD, HN 1975.

Left: SPRING FLOWERS, HN 1807. Center: MARGUERITE, HN 1928. Right: OLIVIA, HN 1995. (Courtesy Doulton & Co., Ltd.)

HN 475
HN 2088
GNOME
   HN 319
   HN 380
   HN 381
CANADIAN MOUNTIE
   HN 321
DIGGER (Australian soldier)
   HN 322
BLIGHTY (English W.W. I soldier)
   HN 323
MOTHER WITH CHILD
   HN 326
   HN 462
   HN 685
   HN 686
   HN 703
   HN 743
   HN 744
   HN 764

A LADY OF THE PERIOD
OF GEORGE III
   HN 331
   HN 444

LADY
   HN 333
   HN 413
   HN 430
   HN 431

HN 447
HN 463 (blue)
HN 465 (blue)
HN 566
HN 678
HN 679
HN 783
HN 793
HN 1211
THE PARSON'S DAUGHTER
   HN 337 (green hat)
   HN 338 (red shawl, hat)
   HN 441
   HN 564
   HN 790
   HN 1242
   HN 1356
   HN 2018 (10″)
IN GRANDMA'S DAYS
   HN 339 (green shawl)
   HN 340 (yellow shawl)
SIR HENRY IRVING AS
CARDINAL WOLSEY. Noke
   HN 344
TONY WELLER
   HN 346
   HN 368
   HN 544
   HN 684
FISHER WOMEN
   HN 349

Left: EASTER DAY, HN 2039 (roses on skirt). Center: DAY DREAMS, HN 1731 (pink). Right: LADY APRIL, HN 1958. (Courtesy Doulton & Co., Ltd.)

HN 359
WOMAN SEATED
HN 351
SOLDIER
HN 353
JAPANESE LADY
HN 354
HN 741
HN 779
HN 1321
HN 1322
DOLLY
HN 355
AN OLD KING
HN 358
HN 623
DOUBLE JESTER. Modeler, Noke
HN 365
CAVALIER
HN 369
BOY ON CROCODILE
HN 373
A GEISHA
HN 376
HN 387
HN 1223
HN 1234
HN 1292
HN 1310
LADY AND BLACKAMOOR
HN 374

HN 375 (yellow)
HN 377 (green)
HN 470
MOOR
HN 378
ELLEN TERRY AS QUEEN
CATHERINE. Noke
HN 379
ST. GEORGE. Designer, F. Thoroughgood
HN 385
HN 386
HN 2067 (L/S)
LADY IN VICTORIAN DRESS
HN 388 (blue)
THE LITTLE MOTHER
HN 389
HN 390
HN 469
HN 1641
A PRINCESS
HN 391(green)
HN 392 (mauve)
HN 420
THE NECKLACE
HN 393
HN 394
HN 428
CONTENTMENT
HN 395
HN 396
HN 421

Left: **POLLY PEACHUM, HN 549.** "Potted"(rose-pink dress with white cap). Right: **VICTORIAN LADY, HN 728.** "Potted" (deep rose dress, blue shawl, lavender bonnet, blue bow). (Collection Mrs. Crayton K. Black.)

Left: **EASTERN LADY,** perfume container, cream, blue and orange; black base, hair, and designs on dress.

Right: **WINDFLOWER, HN 1939.** Cream skirt with pink and blue flower design, rose blouse.

(Collection Mr. & Mrs. Robert M. Fortune.)

Left: **GRANDMA, HN 2052.** Center: **HORNPIPE, HN 2161.** Right: **NEWSBOY, HN 2244.** (Collection Susan Kasulka.)

HN 468
HN 1323
PUFF AND POWDER
  HN 397 (yellow skirt)
  HN 398 (gray skirt)
  HN 400
  HN 432
  HN 433
JAPANESE FAN
  HN 399
  HN 405
  HN 439
  HN 440
MARIE
  HN 401
  HN 434
  HN 502
  HN 504 - 506
BETTY
  HN 402 (red)
  HN 403 (green)
  HN 435 (blue)
  HN 438 (green)
  HN 477
  HN 478

KING CHARLES. Noke
  HN 404
  HN 2084
THE NOSEGAY
  HN 406
  HN 414
  HN 422
  HN 429
  HN 567
  HN 794
OMAR (double figure)
  HN 407
  HN 419
  HN 459
  HN 2247

OMAR KHAYYAM
  HN 408
  HN 409
LADY IN ELIZABETHAN DRESS
  HN 411
MAN IN ELIZABETHAN DRESS
  HN 563
LADY
  HN 413
  HN 447
  HN 463 (blue)
  HN 465
  HN 480-481
  HN 566
  HN 678
  HN 679
  HN 783

HN 793
HN 1211
CHU CHIN CHOW
   HN 417 (with beads)
   HN 418 (sack on shoulder)
THE GOOSE GIRL
   HN 425
   HN 436
   HN 437
   HN 448
   HN 559
   HN 560
LADY WITH MUFF
   HN 443
   HN 748
FRUIT GATHERING (woman and sheep)
   HN 449
   HN 476
   HN 503
   HN 561
   HN 562
   HN 706
   HN 707
OLD MAN SQUATTING
   HN 451
   HN 455
   HN 641
LONDON CRY
   HN 452
MYFANWY JONES
   HN 456
SMILING BUDDHA. Noke
   HN 454
NUDE FIGURE SEATED
   HN 457
LADY WITH SHAWL
   HN 458
REGENCY GENTLEMAN
   HN 464
   HN 753
REGENCY LADY
   HN 754
LADY WITH BOUQUET
   HN 466
   HN 672
   HN 488
BALLOON WOMAN WITH CHILD
   HN 479
   HN 548
   HN 583
FORTY THIEVES
   HN 423-427
   HN 480-484
   HN 490-501
   HN 645-649
   HN 663-667
   HN 712-714
   HN 1336

PEARLY BOY AND PEARLY GIRL, HN 1482, 1483. Black cap and hat, costumes in green, brown, and rust, green scarf and green tie with black dots. (Collection Mr. & Mrs. Robert M. Fortune.)

LEISURE HOUR, HN 2055. See color insert. (Collection Susan Kasulka.)

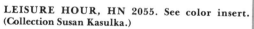

Left: SABBATH MORN, HN 1982 (red). Center: SUNDAY MORN, HN 2189 (red). Right: ROSEMARY, HN 2091 (red). (Collection Susan Kasulka.)

Top left: SYMPHONY, HN 2287; top right: HEART TO HEART, HN 2276. Bottom, left to right: THE CRAFTSMAN, HN 2284; ELEGANCE, HN 2264; RHAPSODY, HN 2267; THE CLOCKMAKER, HN 2279. (Courtesy Doulton & Co., Ltd.)

Group of modern figures. Top: SWEET SIXTEEN, HN 2231; MELODY, HN 2202. Bottom, left to right: TEENAGER, HN 2203; COLUMBINE, HN 2185; HARLEQUIN, HN 2186. (Courtesy Doulton & Co., Ltd.)

GEORGIANA, HN 2093. See color insert. (Collection Susan Kasulka.)

JESTER MASK, HN 1630. (Collection Ron Heberlee.)

Left: DELPHINE, HN 2136 (blue). Center: JEAN, HN 2032 (orange-red, green shawl). Right: GENEVIEVE, HN 1962 (red). (Collection Susan Kasulka.)

HN 1350-54
LADY IN CRINOLINE
 HN 485
 HN 650-655
 HN 695
BALLET DANCER
 HN 487
LITTLE GIRL WITH KITTEN
 HN 507
OLD WOMAN
 HN 513
SENTINEL
 HN 523
LUCKY LOCKET
 HN 524
 HN 693
FLOWER SELLER'S CHILDREN
 HN 525
 HN 551
 HN 1206
 HN 1342
 HN 1406
DICKENS CHINA FIGURES
 Mr. Pickwick. HN 529; HN 556
 The Fat Boy. HN 530; HN 555
 Sam Weller. HN 531
 Mr. Micawber. HN 532; HN 557
 Sairey Gamp. HN 333; HN 558
 Fagin. HN 534
 Pecksniff. HN 535; HN 553
 Stiggins. HN 536
 Bill Sykes. HN 537
 Sergeant Buz Fuz. HN 538
 Tiny Tim. HN 539
 Little Nell. HN 540
 Alred Jingle. HN 541
 Tony Weller. HN 544; HN 684
 Uriah Heep. HN 545; HN 554
 The Artful Dodger. HN 546
THE COBBLER. Modeler, Noke
 HN 542
 HN 543
 HN 681-682
 HN 1251
 HN 1705 (earthenware)
 HN 1706
POLLY PEACHUM (curtseying) Harradir
 HN 549
 HN 550
 HN 694
 HN 698 (pink)
 HN 699 (blue)
 HN 734
WOMAN WITH CHILD IN ARMS
 HN 570
 HN 572
FALSTAFF
 HN 571

HN 575
HN 608
HN 609
HN 618
HN 619
HN 638
HN 1216
HN 1606
HN 2054
MADONNA AND CHILD
    HN 573
    HN 576
    HN 594
    HN 613
CHELSEA PAIR
    HN 577
    HN 578
    HN 579
    HN 580
EASTERN LADY (Grosmith's 'Tsang Hang'
Perfume of Thibet)
    HN 582
BALLOON WOMAN
    HN 583
LADY WITH APPLE
    HN 584
    HN 624
PIERETTE
    HN 585
    HN 635
    HN 642
    HN 643
    HN 644
    HN 691
    HN 711
    HN 795
    HN 721
    HN 731
    HN 732
    HN 738
    HN 796
    HN 1749
    HN 2216
BABY BOY IN TURBAN
    HN 586
    HN 587
    HN 661-662
    HN 1210
    HN 1212-14
    HN 1225
POLLY, BEGGAR'S OPERA
    HN 588-589
    HN 614
MACHEATH, BEGGAR'S OPERA
    HN 590

THE BEGGAR, BEGGAR'S OPERA
    HN 591

Left: PRUE, HN 1990 (red). Center: DELIGHT, HN 1772 (red). Right: DORCAS, HN 1558 (purple). (Collection Susan Kasulka.)

FORTY WINKS, HN 1917. Earthenware figure, 1945-1973. (Courtesy Doulton & Co., Ltd.)

No. 2157
GYPSY DANCE

No. 2147
AUTUMN BREEZES

No. 2148
BRIDESMAID

No. 2156
THE POLKA

Top: GYPSY DANCE, HN 2157 (rare, one hand free). Lower, left to right: AUTUMN BREEZES, HN 2147 (black & yellow); BRIDESMAID, HN 2146; THE POLKA, HN 2156. (Courtesy Doulton & Co., Ltd.)

LILAC TIME   LA SYLPHIDE   GAY MORNING

THE FOREST GLADE   GISELLE   DELPHINE

Top, left to right: LILAC TIME, HN 2137; LA SYLPHIDE, HN 2138; GAY MORNING, HN 2135. Lower, left to right: THE FOREST GLADE, HN 2139; GISELLE, HN 2140; DELPHINE, HN 2136. (Courtesy Doulton & Co., Ltd.)

Left: **CLARISSA, HN 1525.** Green dress, red shawl, orange scarf and hat, blue and red umbrella. Right: **RHODA, HN 1571.** Brown dress, rose bow and hat with green feather, rust shawl with green spots and rose fringe. (Collection Mr. & Mrs. Robert M. Fortune.)

Left: **COPPELIA, HN 2115.** Small figure in blue ballet skirt, red blouse, blue shoes, blonde hair with red flower at each ear. Right: **KATE HARD-CASTLE, HN 1719.** Salmon skirt, gloves, hat ribbon, and flowers; nile green overskirt. (Collection Mr. & Mrs. Robert M. Fortune.)

THE HIGHWAYMAN, BEGGAR'S OPERA
    HN 592
WOMAN CROUCHING
    HN 595
    HN 596
THE BATHER
    HN 597
    HN 687
    HN 773
    HN 774
    HN 781-82
    HN 1238
EASTERN MAN AND WOMAN
    HN 598
THE MASQUERADERS
    HN 599
    HN 600
PRIMROSES
    HN 603
    HN 606
    HN 1617
KING CUPS
    HN 604
    HN 605
    HN 607
POKE BONNET
    HN 612
    HN 765
LADY IN PERIOD DRESS
    HN 615
    HN 628
    HN 637 (gilt)
    HN 690
    HN 700
    HN 708
GENTLEMAN IN PERIOD DRESS
    HN 356
    HN 636 (gilt)
    HN 683
    HN 709
    HN 778
ELF ON ROCK
    HN 621-622
ELSIE MAYNARD
    HN 639
OLD LADY
    HN 640
HARLEQUIN
    HN 656-657
MAMSELLE
    HN 658-659
    HN 724
    HN 786
GIRL GATHERING APPLES
    HN 674
BALLERINA
    HN 676 (swan dance)

Right: WOOD NYMPH, 2192. Left: STAYED AT
HOME, HN 2207. (Courtesy Doulton & Co., Ltd.)

Left: BETSY, HN 2111 (light red). Center:
SUMMER'S DAY, HN 2181(white). Right:
CAROLYN, HN 2116. White with colored flowers.
(Collection Susan Kasulka.)

Left: **RENDEZVOUS** (red) HN 2212, c. 1961-1971.
Right: **ROSEANNA** (pink), HN 1959. (Collection
Susan Kasulka.)

Left: **SKATER, HN 2117** (red). Center: **SWEET
APRIL, HN 2215**(pink). Right: **LADY APRIL, HN
1958** (red). (Collection Susan Kasulka.)

HARLEQUINETTE
  HN 768-769
  HN 780
LADY WITH BOY
  HN 771
BO-PEEP
  HN 777
  HN 1202
GIRL SEATED ON CHAIR
  HN 788
FLOWER GIRL
  HN 789
TÊTE-A-TÊTE
  HN 798-799
  HN 1200
  HN 1236-37
LADY IN RIDING HABIT
  HN 1201
ANGELA
  HN 1204
  HN 1303
MISS 1926
  HN 1205
  HN 1207
PRINCE OF WALES
  HN 1217
NEGLIGEE
  HN 1219
  HN 1228
  HN1272-73
  HN 1454 (pink)
LIDO LADY
  HN 1220
  HN 1229
LADY JESTER
  HN 1221-1222
  HN 1284-85
A WANDERING MINSTREL
  HN 1224
BLUEBIRD
  HN 1280
KO-KO
  HN 1266
  HN 1286
YUM-YUM
  HN 1268
  HN 1287
CARMEN
  HN 1267
  HN 1300
SCOTSMAN
  HN 1269
SWIMMER
  HN 1270
THE MASK
  HN 1271
FAIRY
  HN 1324

Left: PRUDENCE, HN 1883. Figure in blue, green, and white with red in scarf. Right: ROWENA, HN 2077. Underskirt pale green, overskirt rose shading to pink; overblouse deep rose with blue flowers. Black hat with flowers and ribbons of blue, red, and white. (Collection Mr. & Mrs. Robert M. Fortune.)

Left: BONNIE LASSIE, HN 1626. Red shawl and tam, pink skirt. Yellow roses, purple and pink tulips in basket. Right: HERE A LITTLE CHILD I STAND, HN 1546. Barefoot child in blue dress standing on green base. (Collection Mr. & Mrs. Robert M. Fortune.)

Left: **LIZANA, HN 1756.** Spanish dancer in pink skirt, green cape, varicolored shawl, and black hair. Right: **REGENCY BEAU, HN 1972.** Pink suit, green cape, black hat, shoes; white hair, cuff ruffles, and jabot. (Collection Mr. & Mrs. Robert M. Fortune.)

Left: **VICTORIAN LADY, HN 728** (red). Center: **MIDINETTE, HN 2090** (light blue). Right: **MARGUERITE, HN 1928** (pink). (Collection Susan Kasulka.)

HN 1439
SWEET AND TWENTY
    HN 1298
    HN 1360
    HN 1437-38
    HN 1549 (pink)
    HN 1563 (black settee)
    HN 1589
    HN 1610 (small)
SIESTA
    HN 1305
SONNY
    HN 1313-14
OLD BALLOON SELLER
    HN 1315 (woman seated)
TOYS
    HN 1316
SNAKE CHARMER
    HN 1317
SWEET ANNE
    HN 1318
    HN 1330-31
    HN 1453
    HN 1496 (red)
    HN 1631
    HN 1701
ROSAMUND
    HN 1320
    HN 1497
    HN 1551 (blue)
SWIMMER
    HN 1270
    HN 1326
    HN 1329
BO-PEEP
    HN 1327-29
    HN 1810 (blue)
    HN 1811 (pink)
TULIPS
    HN 1334
FOLLY
    HN 1335
    HN 1750
MENDICANT
    HN 1355
    HN 1365
PRISCILLA
    HN 1337 (pink)
    HN 1340
    HN 1495 (blue)
    HN 1501 (orange)
COURTIER
    HN 1338
CONVENT GARDEN
    HN 1339
MARIETTA
    HN 1341
    HN 1446

HN 1699
DULCINEA
HN 1343
HN 1419
SUNSHINE GIRL
HN 1344
HN 1348
IONA
HN 1346
MOIRA
HN 1347
ROSINA
HN 1358
HN 1364
HN 1556
TRINKET SELLER
HN 1361
MASK SELLER
HN 1361
HN 2103
PANTALETTES
HN 1362
HN 1412
HN 1507 (orange)
DOREEN
HN 1363
KITTY
HN 1367
ROSE
HN 1368
HN 1416 (blue)
HN 1506 (orange)
HN 1654 (green)
BOY ON PIG
HN 1369
MARIE
HN 1370
HN 1417 (orange)
HN 1489 (green)
HN 1531 (yel. & green)
HN 1635 (red & blue)
HN 1655 (red)
BETTY
HN 1404-5
HN 1435-36
THE WINNER
HN 1407
JOHN PEEL
HN 1408
HUNTING SQUIRE
HN 1409
ABDULLA
HN 1410
HN 2104
PATRICIA
HN 1414
HN 1430
HN 1462 (green)

Left: NADINE, HN 1886. Pink dress with blue sash and hat, blonde hair. Right: COLLINET, HN 1999. White dress, red-orange cape, blonde hair. (Collection Mr. & Mrs. Robert M. Fortune.)

HN 1567 (red)
PHYLLIS
HN 1420
HN 1430
HN 1486
HN 1698
BARBARA
HN 1421
HN 1432
HN 1461 (green)
JOAN
HN 1422
HN 2023
BABETTE
HN 1423-24
CALUMET
HN 1428
HN 1689
HN 2068
GOSSIPS
HN 1426
HN 1429
HN 2025
BRIDESMAID
HN 1433-34
HN 1530 (yel.)
HN 2148
HN 2196

MISS DEMURE
HN 1402
HN 1440
HN 1463
HN 1499 (pink)
HN 1560
CHILD AND FLOWER STUDY
HN 1441-1443
PAULINE
HN 1444
MARIGOLD
HN 1447
HN 1451
HN 1555
RITA
HN 1448 (red)
HN 1450 (blue)
LITTLE MISTRESS
HN 1449
MOLLY MALONE
HN 1455
ALL A BLOOMING
HN 1457 (or. & blue)
HN 1466 (blue & brown)
MONICA
HN 1458 (green)
HN 1459 (mauve)
HN 1467 (pink & blue)

Left: **CRAFTSMAN, HN 2284.** Right: **TINSMITH, HN 2146. (Collection Susan Kasulka.)**

Left: **CAMELLIA, HN 2222.** Right: **MAS-QUERADE, HN 2251** (blue) also red, **HN 2259.** (Courtesy Doulton & Co., Ltd.)

PAISLEY SHAWL
    HN 1392
    HN 1460 (green)
    HN 1707
    HN 1739
    HN 1914 (M.6 1/2")
    HN 1987 (L.9")
    HN 1988 (M. 6 1/2")
CARPET SELLER
    HN 1464
PAMELA
    HN 1468 (blue)
    HN 1469 (yellow)
    HN 1564 (pink)
CHLOE
    HN 1470 (yel. & red)
    HN 1476 (blue)
    HN 1479
    HN 1498 (yellow)
    HN 1765 (red)
    HN 1956
ANNETTE
    HN 1471 (mauve)
    HN 1472 (green)
    HN 1550
DREAMLAND
    HN 1473 (blue)
    HN 1481 (red)
LOVE IN THE STOCKS
    HN 1474 (red)
    HN 1475 (green)
SYLVIA
    HN 1478
NEWHAVEN FISHWIFE
    HN 1480
PEARLY BOY
    HN 1482 (black hat)
    HN 1548 (red hat)
    HN 2035 (hands clasped)
PEARLY GIRL
    HN 1483 (black hat)
    HN 1549 (red hat)
    HN 2036
JENNIFER
    HN 1484
GRETA
    HN 1485 (pink)
SUZETTE
    HN 1487 (pink)
    HN 1577 (blue)
    HN 1585 (green)
    HN 1696
    HN 2026
GLORIA
    HN 1488
    HN 1700
DORCAS
    HN 1490 (mauve)

HN 1491 (green)
HN 1558 (red)
OLD LAVENDER SELLER
HN 1492 (red & green)
HN 1571
THE POTTER
HN 1493
HN 1518 (green)
HN 1522(black)
GWENDOLINE
HN 1494 (green)
HN 1503 (orange)
HN 1570 (red)
LUCY ANN
HN 1502 (red)
HN 1565 (green)
SWEET MAID
HN 1504 (mauve)
HN 1505 (red)
HELEN
HN 1508 (green)
HN 1509
HN 1572 (red)
CONSTANCE
HN 1510 (blue)
HN 1511 (orange)
DOLLY VARDEN
HN 1514 (red)
HN 1515 (green)
CICELY
HN 1516 (blue)
VERONICA
HN 1517 (red)
HN 1519 (blue)
HN 1650
HN 1915 (8")
HN 1943
EUGENE
HN 1520 (pink)
HN 1521 (red)
LIZETTE
HN 1523 (red)
HN 1524 (blue)
HN 1684
CLARISSA
HN 1525
HN 1687
ANTHEA
HN 1526 (green)
HN 1527 (mauve)
HN 1528
JANET
HN 1537 (red)
HN 1538 (blue)
HN 1652
HN 1737
HN 1916

Left: DANCING YEARS, HN 2235 (blue). Right: DEBUTANTE, HN 2210 (blue). (Collection Susan Kasulka.)

HN 1964 (M/S)
BATHER
HN 1540
BATHER (Happy Joy, Baby Boy)
HN 1541
BATHER (Little Child so Rare & Sweet)
HN 1542
DANCING EYES & SUNNY HAIR
HN 1543
DO YOU WONDER WHERE FAIRIES ARE?
HN 1544
CALLED LOVE; a little boy almost wanton, etc.
HN 1545
HERE A LITTLE CHILD I STAND
HN 1546
PINKIE
HN 1552 (pink)
HN 1553 (blue)
DORCAS
HN 1558
WILLY WON'T HE
HN 1561 (blue)
HN 1584 (red)
GRETCHEN
HN 1562

Upper: HOME AGAIN, HN 2167. Lower: ESMERALDA, HN 2168. (Courtesy Doulton & Co., Ltd.)

73

No. 2053

No. 2052

No. 2056

No. 2051

No. 2054

Top left: THE GAFFER, HN 2053. Right: GRANDMA, HN 2052. Lower, left to right: SUSAN, HN 2056; ST. GEORGE & DRAGON, HN 2051; FALSTAFF, HN 2054. (Courtesy Doulton & Co., Ltd.)

Faraway
Height 2½"

Cookie
Height 5"

Sea Sprite
Height 7½"

Southern Belle
Height 7½"

The Love Letter
Height 5"

Top row, left to right: FARAWAY, HN 2133 (2½ inches); COOKIE, HN 2218 (current); SEA SPRITE, HN 2191, (First introduced c. 1928 as HN 1261, discontinued c. 1962.) Lower left: SOUTHERN BELLE, HN 2229. Right: THE LOVE LETTER, HN 2149 (current). (Courtesy Doulton & Co., Ltd.)

AFTERNOON TEA, HN 1747. (Left figure in
flowered skirt, blue blouse; right figure pink dress,
green shawl, and hat.) (Courtesy Doulton & Co.)

Left: THE SUITOR, HN 2132. Right: A COURT-
ING, HN 2004 (girl light green.) (Collection Susan
Kasulka.)

ESTELLE
    HN 1566
    HN 1802
CHARMIAN
    HN 1568 (red)
    HN 1569 (mar. & green)
    HN 1651
    HN 1948
    HN 1949
RHODA
    HN 1573 (or. & green)
    HN 1574 (or. & black)
    HN 1688
DAISY
    HN 1575
    HN 1961
TILDY
    HN 1576
HINGED PARASOL
    HN 1578 (red)
    HN 1579 (blue)
ROSEBUD
    HN 1580 (pink)
    HN 1581 (white)
MARION
    HN 1582 (green hat)
    HN 1583 (blue hat)
CAMILLE
    HN 1586 (red)
    HN 1648
HENRIETTE
    HN 1587
THE BRIDE
    HN 1588
    HN 1600 (pink)
    HN 1762
    HN 1841
    HN 2166
WALL MASKS
    HN 1590-97
    HN 1601-1604
CLOTILDE
    HN 1598 (yel. & red)
    HN 1599 (blue & red)
THE EMIR
    HN 1605
CERISE
    HN 1607
MASK, BABY
    HN 1608
MASK, JESTER
    HN 1609
    HN 1611
    HN 1630
    HN 1673-74
MASK, GIRL
    HN 1612 (pink)

HN 1613 (green)
HN 1614 (blue)
HN 1658-59
ROSABELLE
HN 1620
IRENE
HN 1621
HN 1697
HN 1952(blue)
EVELYN
HN 1622
HN 1637
BONNIE LASSIE
HN 1626
CURLY NOB
HN 1627
MARGOT
HN 1628 (blue)
HN 1636 (red)
HN 1653 (red & white)
GRIZEL
HN 1629
CLEMENCY
HN 1633 (mauve)
HN 1634 (green)
HN 1643 (red)
LADY BIRD
HN 1638 (pink)
HN 1640 (blue)
DAINTY MAY
HN 1638 (pink)
HN 1656 (mauve)
GRANNY'S SHAWL
HN 1642
HN 1647
HERMINA
HN 1644 (white)
HN 1646 (red)
HN 1704
HN 2058
AILEEN
HN 1645
HN 1664
HN 1803
DELICIA
HN 1662 (red)
HN 1663 (mauve)
HN 1681
MISS WINSOME
HN 1665 (mauve)
HN 1666 (green)
BLOSSOM
HN 1667
SIBELL
HN 1668
HN 1695
HN 1735

BALLERINA, HN 2116. Pale pink with blue ribbons and roses. (Courtesy Doulton & Co., Ltd.)

THE BASKET WEAVER, HN 2245, c. 1959-1962. (Collection Susan Kasulka.)

Left: CRADLE SONG, HN 2246 (blue-brown).
Right: FIRST STEPS, HN 2242 (blue). (Collection Susan Kasulka.)

Left to right: ANTHEA, HN 1527, "Potted." PAMELA, HN 1468, "Potted." SHY ANNE, HN 64, "Potted." Child figure on pedestal. (Collection Wanda Wempe.)

BABIE
    HN 1679
    HN 1842
GILLIAN
    HN 1670
TERESA
    HN 1682 (red)
    HN 1683 (blue)
CYNTHIA
    HN 1685 (pink)
    HN 1686 (blue)
JUNE
    HN 1690 (green)
    HN 1691 (pink)
    HN 1947
    HN 2027
SONIA
    HN 1692
    HN 1738
VIRGINIA
    HN 1693
    HN 1694 (green)
CAMILLA
    HN 1710 (pink)
    HN 1711 (green)
    HN 2222
DAFFY DOWN DILLY
    HN 1712 (green)
    HN 1713 (blue)
MILLICENT
    HN 1714 (red)
    HN 1715 (mauve)
    HN 1860
DIANA
    HN 1716 (pink & blue)
    HN 1717 (green)
    HN 1986
KATE HARDCASTLE
    HN 1718 (pink & green)
    HN 1719 (red & green)
    HN 1734 (green)
    HN 1861
    HN 1919
    HN 2028
FRANGOON
    HN 1720 (multicolor)
    HN 1721 (green)
COMING OF SPRING
    HN 1722 (pink)
    HN 1723 (green)
RUBY
    HN 1724 (red & mauve)
    HN 1725 (blue)
CELIA
    HN 1726 (pink)
    HN 1727 (green)

Top, left to right: ROSEMARY, HN 2091 (red); MIDINETTE, HN 2090, (lavender); SWEET MAID, HN 2092 (blue); JUDITH, HN 2089 (red).

Lower row, left to right: UNCLE NED, NH 2094; IBRAHIM, HN 2095; GEORGIANA, HN 2093. (Courtesy Doulton & Co., Ltd.)

THE NEW BONNET
  HN 1728
  HN 1957
VERA
  HN 1729 (pink)
  HN 1730 (green)
DAY DREAMS
  HN 1731 (pink)
  HN 1732 (blue)
  HN 1944
FRIAR OF ORDERS
  HN 1733 (gray)
GLADYS (bust)
  HN 1740 (green)
  HN 1741 (pink)
SIR WALTER RALEIGH
  HN 1742 (china)
  HN 1751 (earthenware)
MIRABEL
  HN 1743 (blue)
  HN 1744 (pink)
THE RUSTIC SWAIN
  HN 1745
  HN 1746
AFTERNOON TEA
  HN 1747
  HN 1748
REGENCY
  HN 1752

ELEANOR
  HN 1753
  HN 1754
THE COURT SHOEMAKER
  HN 1755

LIZANA
  HN 1756
  HN 1761
ROMANY SUE
  HN 1757 (green)
  HN 1758 (mauve)
ORANGE LADY
  HN 1759 (plaid)
  HN 1953 (green)
FOUR O'CLOCK
  HN 1760
WINDFLOWER
  HN 1763 (red)
  HN 1764 (blue)
  HN 1920
  HN 1939 (7½")
  HN 2029
NANA
  HN 1766 (red)
  HN 1767 (mauve)
IVY
  HN 1768
  HN 1769

MAUREEN
  HN 1770 (pink)
  HN 1771 (blue)
DELIGHT
  HN 1772 (pink)
  HN 1773 (blue)
SALOME
  HN 1775
  HN 1826
SPIRIT OF THE WIND
  HN 1777
  HN 1825
WEST WIND
  HN 1776
  HN 1826
BEETHOVEN
  HN 1778
MACAW
  HN 1779
  HN 1829
LADY OF THE SNOWS
  HN 1780
  HN 1830
MASK - LION OF THE EAST
  HN 1781
  HN 1784
MASK - FATE
  HN 1782
  HN 1785

MASK - ST. AGNES
  HN 1783
  HN 1786
  HN 1787-90
OLD BALLOON SELLER AND DOGGY
  HN 1791
HENRY VII
  HN 1792
THIS LITTLE PIG
  HN 1793 (red)
  HN 1794 (blue)
MY LADY'S MAID
  HN 1795
  HN 1821 (green)
  HN 1822
HAZEL
  HN 1796 (green)
  HN 1797 (pink)
LILY
  HN 1798 (pink)
  HN 1799 (green)
GRANNY
  HN 1804
  HN 1832 (pink)
TO BED
  HN 1805
  HN 1806
SPRING FLOWERS
  HN 1807
  HN 1945
CISSIE
  HN 1808
  HN 1809
FORGET-ME-NOT
  HN 1812 (pink)
  HN 1813 (blue)
MASK — POMPADOUR
  HN 1816-17
  HN 1823-24
MIRANDA
  HN 1818 (pink & green)
  HN 1819 (pink & blue)
REFLECTIONS
  HN 1820 (pink)
  HN 1847 (red)
  HN 1848 (blue & green)
THE CLOUD
  HN 1831
TOP O' THE HILL
  HN 1833 (green)
  HN 1834 (red)
  HN 1849 (pink)
VERENA
  HN 1835
  HN 1854
VANESSA
  HN 1836

HN 1838
MARGUERITE
  HN 1837
  HN 1928
  HN 1946
CHRISTINE
  HN 1839 (mauve)
  HN 1840 (pink)
BIDDY PENNY FARTHING
  HN 1843
MODENA
  HN 1845
  HN 1846
  HN 1854 (pink)
ANTOINETTE
  HN 1850 (pink)
  HN 2326
MEMORIES
  HN 1855 (pink)
  HN 1856 (blue)
  HN 1857 (pink & blue)
DAWN
  HN 1858
JASMINE
  HN 1862 (blue)
  HN 1863 (green)
  HN 1876
SWEET AND FAIR
  HN 1864 (blue shawl)
  HN 1865 (gold shawl)
WEDDING MORN
  HN 1866 (cream)
  HN 1867 (pink)
DRYAD OF THE PINES
  HN 1869
LITTLE LADY MAKE BELIEVE
  HN 1870
ANNABELLA
  HN 1871 (pink)
  HN 1872 (blue)
  HN 1875 (pink)
GRANNY'S HERITAGE
  HN 1873 (pink)
  HN 1874 (blue 61/4")
JEAN
  HN 1877 (blue)
  HN 1878 (red)
  HN 2032
BON JOUR
  HN 1879
  HN 1888 (pink)
NELL GWYNNE
  HN 1882
  HN 1887 (pink)
PRUDENCE
  HN 1883 (blue)
  HN 1884 (pink)

Top row, left to right: **MIDSUMMER NOON, HN 2033; JANET, HN 1537** (red); **LYDIA, HN 1908** (red). Lower row, left to right: **PATCHWORK QUILT, HN 1984; HER LADYSHIP, HN 1977; GRANNY'S HERITAGE, HN 2031.** (Courtesy Doulton & Co., Ltd.)

Left   AUTUMN BREEZES, HN 1911 (pink with green coat and bonnet).
Center: MARKET DAY, HN 1991. Right: TOP O' THE HILL, HN 1834 (red). (Courtesy Doulton & Co., Ltd.)

NADINE
    HN 1885 (blue)
    HN 1886 (pink)
GOODY TWO SHOES
    HN 1889
    HN 1905
    HN 2037
LAMBING TIME
    HN 1890 (8½")
MISS FORTUNE
    HN 1897 (pink)
    HN 1898 (blue)
MIDSUMMER NOON
    HN 1900 (blue)
    HN 1904 (blue)
PENELOPE
    HN 1901 (pink)
    HN 1904 (blue)
LYDIA
    HN 1906 (blue)
    HN 1907 (green)
    HN 1963 (pink, green shawl)
AUTUMN BREEZES
    HN 1911 (green coat, bonnet)
    HN 1913 (green dress)
    HN 1954 (red)
    HN 2147 (bl. & yel.)

MERYLL
    HN 1917
ROSEANNA
    HN 1921
    HN 1926 (pink)
SWEET SUZY
    HN 1918
SPRING MORNING
    HN 1922 (pink coat)
    HN 1923 (green coat)
FIONA
    HN 1924 (pink)
    HN 1925 (blue)
    HN 1933
THE AWAKENING
    HN 1927
MARGUERITE
    HN 1928 (pink & red)
    HN 1929 (pink)
    HN 1930 (blue)
    HN 1946
MERIEL
    HN 1931 (pink)
    HN 1932 (green)
SWEETING
    HN 1935

MISS MUFFET
    HN 1936 (red coat)
    HN 1937 (green coat)
ANTOINETTE
    HN 1940
PEGGY
    HN 1941
    HN 2038
PYJAMS
    HN 1942
LADY CHARMIAN
    HN 1948 (green)
    HN 1949 (pink)
CLARIBEL
    HN 1950 (blue)
    HN 1951 (red)
BALLOON MAN
    HN 1954
LAVINIA
    HN 1955
LADY APRIL
    HN 1958
    HN 1965
THE CHOICE
    HN 1959 (red)
    HN 1960 (multicolor)

GENEVIEVE
HN 1962
LADY BETTY
HN 1967 (red)
MILADY
HN 1970
SPRINGTIME
HN 1971
REGENCY BEAU
HN 1972
THE CORINTHIAN
HN 1973
EASTER DAY
HN 1976 (lavender)
HN 2039
HER LADYSHIP
HN 1977 (Paisley)
BEDTIME
HN 1978
GOLLYWOG
HN 1979
HN 2040
THE ERMINE COAT
HN 1981
GWYNETH
HN 1980

SABBATH MORN
HN 1982
ROSEBUD
HN 1983
PATCHWORK QUILT
HN 1984
MARGARET
HN 1989

MARY JANE
HN 1990
MARKET DAY
HN 1991
CHRISTMAS MORN
HN 1992

GRISELDA
HN 1993
KAREN
HN 1994 (red, wh. gloves and jabot)
OLIVIA
HN 1995 (lt. bl. dress, multicolored
cape)
PRUE
HN 1996 (peasant cap, apron and laced
basque)
BELLE O' THE BALL
HN 1997 (lady in powered wig, red
costume, seated on Louis XV sofa)
COLINETTE
HN 1998 (green cloak)
HN 1999 (red cloak)

JACQUELINE
HN 2000 (mauve)
HN 2001 (orange)
BESS
HN 2002 (red cape, flowered dress)
HN 2003 (blue cape, red lining, pink
dress, no pattern)
A COURTING
HN 2004 (couple, girl in reds, boy in
blues, tricornered hat)
ANGELINA
HN 2013
JANE
HN 2014
SILKS AND RIBBONS
HN 2017 (old lady peddler selling
multicolor ribbons and materials)
MINUET
HN 2019 (white)
HN 2066 (red)
JANICE
HN 2022 (green)
HN 2165 (black)
DARBY
HN 2024
GRANNY'S HERITAGE
HN 2031
MEMORIES
HN 2030
BROKEN LANCE
HN 2041
OWD WILLUM. (Harradine model)
HN 2042
THE POACHER
HN 2044
MARY, MARY
HN 2044
SHE LOVES ME NOT
HN 2045
HE LOVES ME
HN 2046
ONCE UPON A TIME
HN 2047
MARY HAD A LITTLE LAMB
HN 2048
CURLY LOCKS
HN 2049
WEE WILLIE WINKIE
HN 2050
ST. GEORGE AND THE DRAGON
HN 2051
GRANDMA
HN 2052
THE GAFFER
HN 2053
THE LEISURE HOUR
HN 2055

Left: SUZETTE, HN 1487. Right: PEGGY, HN 1941. (Courtesy Doulton & Co., Ltd.)

BESS, HN 2003 (blue). (Also crimson with flowered skirt, HN 2002.) (Courtesy Doulton & Co., Ltd.)

SUSAN
   HN 2056
JERSEY MILKMAID
   HN 2057
THE BEDTIME STORY
   HN 2059
JACK
   HN 2060
JILL
   HN 2061
LITTLE BOY BLUE
   HN 2062
LITTLE JACK HORNER
   HN 2063
MY PRETTY MAID
   HN 2064
THE FARMER'S WIFE
   HN 2069
BRIDGET
   HN 2070
BERNICE
   HN 2071
THE ROCKING HORSE
   HN 2072
VIVIENNE
   HN 2073
MARIANNE
   HN 2074
FRENCH PEASANT
   HN 2075
PROMENADE
   HN 2076
ROWENA
   HN 2078
DAMARIS
   HN 2079
THE MOOR
   HN 2082
JUDITH
   HN 2089
ROSEMARY
   HN 2091 (red)
SWEET MAID
   HN 2092(mauve)
GEORGIANA
   HN 2093(blue dress, flowered border; red bodice, overskirt. Ribbon & feather headdress)
UNCLE NED
   HN 2094
IBRAHIM
   HN 2095 (Eastern figure, orange & yellow)
LINDA
   HN 2106
VALERIE
   HN 2107

84

BABY BUNTING
    HN 2108

WENDY
    HN 2109 (blue)

CHRISTMAS TIME
    HN 2110 (red)

BETSY
    HN 2111(mauve with flowered apron)

CAROLYN
    HN 2112 (green bodice, gloves; white skirt, pink flowers)

MAYTIME
    HN 2113 (pink with blue scarf and ribbons)

SLEEPY HEAD
    HN 2114 (child with teddy bear, sitting in armchair)

COPPELIA
    HN 2115 (girl in ballet costume, on toes on book; red & blue)

BALLERINA
    HN 2116 (long ballet costume, pale pink & blue)

THE SKATER
    HN 2117 (red)

GOOD KING WENCESLAS (orange with dark purple cape)
    HN 2118

TOWN CRIER
    HN 2119 (red, or., green & black)

GAY MORNING
    HN 2125

RIVER BOY
    HN 2128

THE SUITOR
    HN 2132

FARAWAY
    HN 2133

OLD KING
    HN 2134

DELPHINE
    HN 2136

LILAC TIME
    HN 2137

LA SYLPHIDE
    HN 2138 (pink & blue)

FOREST GLADE
    HN 2139 (white with blue scarf)

BEDTIME STORY, HN 2059.

HERMOINE, HN 2058 (mauve & green); **MINUET, HN 2019** (blue with white dots). **HN 2066** (red). (Courtesy Doulton & Co., Ltd.)

2069
FARMERS WIFE

2070 BRIDGET

2073
VIVIENNE

2072
ROCKING HORSE

2076
PROMENADE

Top row, left: FARMER'S WIFE, HN 2069. Right: BRIDGET, HN 2070. Lower row, left to right: VIVIENNE, HN 2073; ROCKING HORSE, HN 2072; PROMENADE, HN 2076. (All discontinued.) (Courtesy Doulton & Co., Ltd.)

Top row, left to right: MARY JANE, HN 1990; PRUE, HN 1996; MARKET DAY, HN 1991; CHRISTMAS MORN, HN 1992. Lower row, left to right: OLIVIA, HN 1995; BELL O' THE BALL, HN 1997; MARGARET, HN 1989. (Courtesy Doulton & Co., Ltd.)

GISELLE
  HN 2140 (figure in blue & pink sitting
  on bench)
RAG DOLL
  HN 2142
FRIAR TRUCK
  HN 2143
JOVIAL MONK
  HN 2144
WARDROBE MISTRESS
  HN 2145
THE TINSMITH
  HN 2146
THE LOVE LETTER
  HN 2149 (figures in pink & blue sitting
  on sofa)
WILLY WON'T HE
  HN 2150
MOTHER'S HELPER
  HN 2151
ADRIENNE
  HN 2152 (purple)
  HN 2304 (blue)
THE ONE THAT GOT AWAY
  HN 2153
CHILD FROM WILLIAMSBURG
  HN 2154
POLKA
  HN 2156
GYPSY DANCE
  HN 2157
  HN 2230
ALICE
  HN 2158
FORTUNE TELLER
  HN 2159
APPLE MAID
  HN 2160
HORNPIPE
  HN 2161
THE FOAMING QUART
  HN 2162
IN THE STOCKS
  HN 2162
HOME AGAIN
  HN 2167
ESMERALDA
  HN 2168
DIMITY
  HN 2169
INVITATION
  HN 2170
FIDDLER
  HN 2171
JOLLY SAILOR
  HN 2172

THE ORGAN GRINDER
  HN 2173
THE TAILOR
  HN 2174
THE BEGGAR
  HN 2175
MY TEDDY
  HN 2177
ENCHANTMENT
  HN 2178
NOELLE
  HN 2179
SUMMER'S DAY
  HN 2181
SUNDAY MORNING
  HN 2184
COLUMBINE
  HN 2185
HARLEQUIN
  HN 2186
WOOD NYMPH
  HN 2192
FAIR LADY
  HN 2193
MELODY
  HN 2202
TEENAGER
  HN 2203
LONG JOHN SILVER
  HN 2204
MASTER SWEEP
  HN 2205
STAYED AT HOME
  HN 2207
SILVERSMITH OF WILLIAMSBURG
  HN 2208
HOSTESS OF WILLIAMSBURG
  HN 2209
DEBUTANTE
  HN 2210
FAIR MAIDEN
  HN 2211
RENDEZVOUS
  HN 2212
BUNNY
  HN 2214
SWEET APRIL
  HN 2215
OLD KING COLE
  HN 2217
COOKIE
  HN 2218
WINSOME
  HN 2220

From this date on, c. 1970, there are Royal Doulton catalogs that give accurate numbers and dates up to the present production.

III. Royal Doulton Animal Figures

Figures of animals and birds offer an interesting field for the collector. There are many of these figures available. The Doulton Potteries have produced models of animals and birds for several generations, beginning with the early salt-glazed stoneware whimsical sculptures of mice and frogs by George Tinworth which were produced at Lambeth in the 1880s.

Between 1909 and 1914, Charles J. Noke modeled and produced a group of animals, both naturalistic and stylized, including lions, elephants, tigers, foxes, rabbits, ducks, penguins, pigs, dogs, and cats. More animal figures were added between 1914 and 1917. George Fernyhough painted some of the early models up to 1905, and Eric Webster painted the majority of those after 1910 and 1963.

A small group of early animals and bird figures was illustrated in a catalog of the late 1930s. These included:

Penguin, 6½ inches, HN 882
Mallard, 5 inches, HN 956
Aberdeen Terrier, 3½ inches, HN 980 (standing)
Hare, 3 inches, HN 979 (lying down)
Fox, 5 inches, HN 147/12 (sitting)
Alsatian, 8 inches, HN 921 (sitting)
English Setter, 6 inches HN 976 (sitting)
Tiger, 7 inches HN 912 (sitting, head turned)
Terrier, 6 inches, HN 914

Later there were figures of many other both wild and tame animals, including cockerels, dolphins, elephants, ibex, kangaroos, bears, pelicans, pigeons, rabbits, and squirrels. These were designed by various artists for reproduction from molds. Many were produced in salt-glazed stoneware at Lambeth, and the later popular figures of bone china cats and dogs were produced at Burslem. In addition to separate figures there were small figures used as decoration on ashtrays, bookends, matchbox holders and ring stands.

In the 1950 catalog over twenty-five sundry animals and birds were listed. These included playful miniature cats and kittens such as the kitten playing with its tail and the tiny laughing kitten, Lucky. There is also a larger Persian cat and, a few years later, several figures of Siamese cats were added. There are also playful figures of dogs with a ball or an old slipper, dogs yawning, begging, and eating from a saucer.

Royal Doulton never put out a separate catalog of dogs, but dogs and other animals are included in many catalogs along with figurines.

There are long lists of dogs in the catalogs of 1950 and 1959, and *Collector's Book No. 7, 1961,* has many pages of illustrations. These include a page of tiny kittens with the early Persian cat, HN 999; the Siamese cats and other animals of the Chatcull Range; two pages of miniature dogs and six figures of miniature pigs; a page of Dogs of Character; dogs in a basket; and a page of penguins, a tiny duck, rabbits, and Lucky the cat. There are four pages of Championship Dogs and the Cocker with Pheasant and the English Setter with Pheasant. Doulton listed their dogs in several different categories, and these different class divisions are continued in the catalog listings, today. They are Champion Dogs, Character Dogs, and Miniature Dogs.

Bulldog, brindled. L, HN 1042.

Champion Alsatian, "Benign of Picardy." L, HN 1115.

Bulldogs. S/M/L (Collection Ann Cook.)

Champion Dogs

In the late 1930s Royal Doulton introduced their range of Champion Dogs. These dogs were modeled by Frederick T. Daws and later by Margeret Davies. These dogs are actual portraits modeled from life. Some models are of named champions whose owners have approved them as perfect likenesses of their dogs. The breeds include Alsatian, Airedale, Bull Terrier, Cocker Spaniel, Dalmation, Dachshund. English Setter, Foxhound, Rough-haired Terrier, Smooth-haired Terrier, Scottish Terrier, Irish Setter, West Highland Terrier, Cairn, Collie, Greyhound, Sealyham, and Pekingese. Later additions include the Doberman Pinscher, Boxer, Labrador, and the Welsh Corgi. As other breeds such as the French Poodle became popular, they were also produced by Royal Doulton.

Photographs: Doulton & Co., Ltd.

Champion Scotch Terrier "Albourne Arthur." M, HN 1015.

Champion Springer Spaniel, "Dry Toast." M, HN 2516.

Champion Dalmation, "Goworth Victor." M, HN 1113.

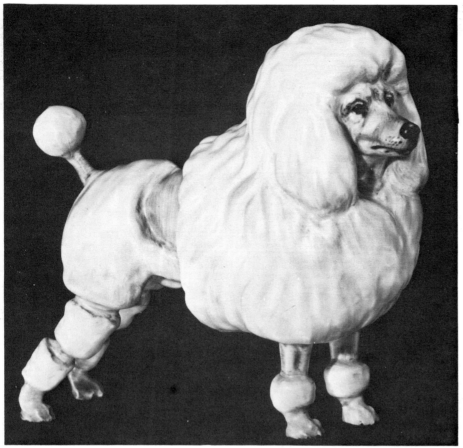

French Poodle, HN 2631. 5½ inches.

Photographs: Doulton & Co., Ltd.

Champion Dachshund "Shrew Saint." Black, M, HN 1128.

Champion Cocker Spaniel, "Lucky Stare of Ware," L, HN 1000.

The following is a list of Royal Doulton Champion Dog models taken from the catalog of September 15, 1950:

Airedale, "Cotsford Topsail"
    L. 1022   M. 1023   S. 1024
Alsatian, "Benign of Picardy"
    L. 1115   M. 1116   S. 1117
American Foxhound
    L. 2524   M. 2525
Bulldog, brindled
    L. 1042   M. 1043   S. 1044
Bulldog, brown and white
    L. 1045   M. 1046   S. 1047
Bulldog, white
    L. 1072   M. 1073   S. 1074
Cairn, "Charming Eyes"
    L. 1033   M. 1034   S. 1035
Cocker Spaniel, liver & white
    L. 1002   M. 1036   S. 1037
Cocker Spaniel, "Lucky Star of Ware"
    L. 1000   M. 1020   S. 1021
Cocker Spaniel, black & white
    L. 1108   M. 1109   S. 1078
Cocker Spaniel, golden
    L. 1186   M. 1187   S. 1188
Cocker & Pheasant, liver & white
    L. 1001   M. 1028   S. 1029
Cocker & Pheasant, b & w
    L. 1137   M. 1138   S. 1062
Collie, "Ashstead Applause"
    L. 1057   M. 1058   S. 1059
Dachshund, all brown
    L. 1139   M. 1140   S. 1141
Dachshund, B, "Shrewd Saint"
    L. 1127   M. 1128   S. 1129
Dalmatian, "Goworth Victor"
    L. 1111   M. 1113   S. 1114
English Setter, "Maeaydd Mustard"
    L. 1049   M. 1050   S. 1051
Foxhound, "Tring Rattler"
    L. 1025   M. 1026   S. 1027
Gordon Setter
    L. 1079   M. 1080   S. 1081

**Setters: Large English Setter, HN 1049. Medium
Gordon Setter, HN 1080; Irish Setter, HN 1056.**

Collection of Mrs. Ann Cook.

Great Dane, American
    L. 2601   M. 2602
Greyhound, brown
    L. 1065   M. 1066   S. 1067
Greyhound
    L. 1075   M. 1076   S. 1077

Irish Setter
    L. 1054   M. 1055   S. 1056
Rough-haired terrier, "Crackley Starter"
    L. 1007   M. 1013   S. 1014
Scotch Terrier, "Albourne Arthur"
    L. 1008   M. 1-15   S. 1016
Sealyham, "Scotia Stylist"
    L. 1030   M. 1031   S. 1032
Springer Spaniel, "Dry Toast"
    L. 2515   M. 2516   S. 2517

Welsh Corgi, "Spring Robin"
    L. 2557   M. 2558   S. 2559
Bull Terrier, white
    M. only   1132
Bull Terrier, brown & white
    M. only   1143
French Poodle
    M. only   2631
Great Dane, "Rebeller of Ouborough"
    M. only   2561

Pekingese, "Biddee of Ifield"
    L. 1011   S. 1012
Smooth-haired Terrier, "Chosen Don of Notts"
    M. 2513
Smooth-haired Terrier
    M. 1069
English Setter & Pheasant
    L. 2529
Pointer
    L. 2624

**Left: Champion Spaniel, liver & white. L,1002.
Right: Greyhound, brown, L, 1065.**

Photographs: Doulton & Co., Ltd.

In the catalog of January 1, 1959, a boxer, "Warlord of Mazelaine,"
Medium, 2643, and a doberman pinscher, "Rancho Dobe's Storm,"
medium, 2645, were added to the listings. Many of these dogs have later
been discontinued, and the price list of February 1, 1976, gives a much
smaller listing.

Left: English Foxhound, HN 1027, S. Right: American Foxhound, M. HN 2525.

Bull Terrier, brindle and white. M, HN 114.

Greyhound, brindle, M. HN 1066; small Dachshunds, left, black, HN 1129; right, brown, HN 1141.

Cocker Spaniels: L, HN 1108; M, HN 1109 (current); S, HN 1072.

Plate with Greyhounds from Falconer Series, D 3696. Brindle Greyhound, M, HN 1066. *Photographs: Ann Cook collection*

Cocker Spaniels: liver and white, L. HN 1002; M. HN 1036; S. HN 1037. Square plate with head of Cocker Spaniel.

Welsh Corgi, Spring Robin. L, HN 2557, M, HN 2558, S, HN 2559 (current).

Cecil Aldin plate, Cecil Aldin pitcher. Character Dog, HN 1100.

Photographs: Ann Cook collection

Three discontinued dogs from Mini Series. Left: white Bull Terrier, K 14; Airedale, K 5; Sealyham, K 4.

Group of medium-sized discontinued dogs: Back row, left to right: Greyhound (brown), HN 1066; English Foxhound, HN 1026; Corgi, HN 2556; Gordon Setter, HN 1080; Bull Terrier (brown and white), HN 1043.

Photographs: Ann Cook collection

Alsatians. Large, HN 1115; Medium, HN 1116 (current); small, HN 1117.

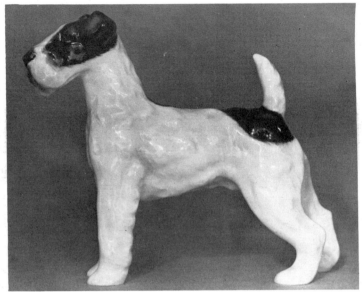

Terrier (rough haired). M, HN 964.

All discontinued Doulton Sealyhams. Champion Series. Right to left: Large, HN 1030; Medium, HN 1031; Small, HN 1032. Square plate with dog's head. Front row, left to right: Mini Sealyhams. Sitting K 3 (current); lying, K 4. Sealyham Character Dogs: sitting, HN 2508; standing, HN 2509; rolling, HN 1098. Sealyham Head Mask, K 27.

Dogs of Character

English Setter & Pheasant, HN 2529. (Current.)

Photographs: Doulton & Co., Ltd.

Character Dogs are figures of dogs in action — running, walking, sitting, or playing with a ball or bone. Those listed in the catalog of 1950 include the following:

Many of these character dogs have been discontinued, and there are only six models listed in the price list of February 1, 1976.

There were also a great number of miniature models of dogs. The list in the 1950 catalog includes the following:

Bulldog . . . . K 1
Bull Pup. . . . . K 2
Sealyham . . . . K 3
Sealyham (lying) . . . . K 4
Airedale. . . . . K 5
Pekingese . . . . K 6
Foxhound . . . . K 7
Terrier . . . . K 8
Cocker Spaniel . . . . K 9
Scotch Terrier . . . . K 10
Cairn . . . . K 11
Alsatian . . . . K 13
Bull Terrier . . . . K 14
Chow Chow . . . . K 15
Welsh Corgi. . . . . K 16
Dachsund. . . . . K 17
Scotch Terrier . . . . K 18
St. Bernard . . . . K 19

Although some of these models have been discontinued, there are still fifteen listed in the 1976 catalog.

There are also plates with dogs, and some of these are signed by the well-known water color artist Cecil Aldin, R.A. (1870-1935). Aldin also probably did some of the designs for dog models and for the series, Aldin's Dogs.

There are several figures of animals that come under the heading of novelties. Lucky, the little black cat, K 12, is a favorite with cat lovers. The Huntsman Fox is also a favorite. An earlier figure of a fox, 100, dressed in a red coat and white tie has long since been discontinued. It was titled Red Fox Coat. In the catalog of January 1, 1960, the figure Union Jack Bull Dog was listed in two sizes, Large 6406 and small, 6407. This figure is said to caricature Winston Churchill. The figure was also made in medium size. The figures are now discontinued and, although not of Doulton's best production, they are collectors' items. The figures of the little Piglets are also collectors' items.

Royal Doulton animal figures are marked with the Doulton trademark and the number of the animal. The numbers reserved for animals include numbers 100 through 299 and 800 through 1199. The majority of the Champion Dog models are numbered 2500 through 2600. Miniature figures are given numbers preceded by the letter "K".

The following is a list of discontinued dogs and horses compiled by the collector, Mrs. Ann Cook.

Fox, Red Coat. D6448. (Current.)

Small Size
Alsatian, 1117
Airedale, 1024
Bulldog, 1044
Cocker, Bl. 1021
Cocker, sitting RW 1029
Cocker, RW 1037
Cocker, BW 1078
Cocker, Red 1188
Collie, 1059
Dachshund, B&T 1129
Dachshund, Red 1141
Dalmatian, 1112

English Setter, 1051
Foxhound, Eng., 1026
Irish Setter, 1056
Sealyham, 1032

Medium Size

Bulldog, Brindle 1043
Bulldog, White 1073
Bull Terrier, Brindle 1143
Corgi, 2558
Dachshund, Red 1140
Foxhound, Am., 2525
Greyhound, Brindle 1066
Gordon Setter, 1080
Sealyham, 1031

Large Size

Alsatian, 1115
Bulldog, B&W 1045
Cocker, R&W 1002
Cocker, B&W 1108
Corgi, 2267
Eng. Setter, 1049
Sealyham, 1030

Bulldog Union Jack. L/M/S.

Red Fox Coat. HN 100.

Photographs: Stadler Co.

**Dogs of Character. Left: HN 2511. Center: HN 1101.
Right: HN 1100.**

99

Groups	Sealyham, K-4	10½" Spaniel, R&W
	Airedale, K-5	10½" Scottish Terrier
Cockers, R&W	Bull Terrier, K-14	10½" Eng. Setter
English Setters		
Alsatians	Other	Horses
Sealyhams		
Cockers, B&W	Sealyham Head Plaque, K-27	Shire Walking, 2564
Corgi	Fox Terrier, Wire, 964	Shire Cantering, 2623 (horse only)
Bulldogs (assorted colors)	Jug w/Foxhounds s/Aldin	Chestnut Mare, 2566
		Thoroughbred Colt, 2571 (Merely a Minor)
Character Dogs	Plates	Pride of the Shires, 2528
Bull Terrier, 1100	Set of 5 head studies:	Sealyhams
Bull Terrier, 2511	Cocker	
Sealyham, 1098	Labrador	Champion Series, large, med. small
Sealyham, 2508	Eng. Setter	Character Series, 1098, 2508, 2509
Sealyham, 2509	Irish Setter	Miniatures, K-3, K-4
	Sealyham	Head Plaque, K-27
Miniature Dogs	10½" Terriers, s/Aldin	Head Portrait Plate

Miniature Dogs. Left to right: Scotch Terrier, K 10; Pekingese, K6; Bull Pup, K2; Terrier, K8; Cocker Spaniel, K 9; Chow K 15.

Miniature Dogs. Left to right: Terrier, K 8; Bulldog, K 2; Foxhound, K 7; Airedale, K 5; Cairn, K 11; Cocker Spaniel, K 9.

Royal Doulton
Horse Models

Pride of the Shires, HN 2528, 9 inches. (Courtesy Doulton & Co., Ltd.)

In the late 1940s Royal Doulton produced a group of horses which were modeled by W.M. Chance. The most famous of these horses was the Royal Steeplechases, "Monaveen," which was made for Queen Elizabeth II (then Princess Elizabeth) in 1949. This horse was painted by Eric Webster, who also painted other horse and animal figures.

The other horse models made at about this date were illustrated in a catalog of the time. They are listed in the catalogs of January 1, 1950, September 15, 1950, and January 1, 1959. The list, taken from the 1950 catalog, is as follows:

Chestnut Mare l/s, 2522 (6½ inches)
Chestnut Mare, small size, 2533
Gude Grey Mare, large size, 2519 (5 inches)
Gude Grey Mare, medium size, no foal, 2569
Gude Grey Mare, small size, no foal, 2570
Farmer's Boy, 2520 (8½ inches)
Farmer's Boy (horse only), 2623
Merely a Minor, medium size, chestnut, 2537
Merely a Minor, small size, chestnut, 2571
Merely a Minor, small size, gray, 2567
Pride of the Shires, large size, gray, 2523
Pride of the Shires, large size, brown, 2528 (9 inches)
Pride of the Shires, small size, brown, no foal, 2564

In the earlier catalog there is an illustration of Merely a Minor, 12 inches, HN 2530. This is not included in the later catalog lists, so must have been discontinued and thus, must be rare. All figures are mounted on grassy turf bases. The Pride of the Shires is the favorite with collectors.

Pride of the Shires was introduced in the 1930s in an open edition, but there is no record of how many were produced. The letter "C" for Chance is the code letter of the designer. The model was discontinued in 1959, and all horse models were discontinued in December, 1966.

The Gude Grey Mare, HN 2519. (Courtesy of Doulton & Co., Ltd.)

The Gude Grey Mare, 2519, lighter colors. (Courtesy Doulton Co., Ltd.)

Left: Dapple Grey, HN 2521, 7 1/8 inches. Right: Farmer's Boy, HN 2520, 9¼ inches. (Courtesy Doulton & Co., Ltd.)

The Chatcull
Range of Animals

Brown Bear, HN 2059.

The Chatcull Range of animals was introduced by Royal Doulton January 1, 1940, and the complete list of animal figures produced is given in the catalog of the same date. This series was designed by J.W. Ledger. The animals are modeled in modern, stylized form with low-key coloring and simple lines. There is a wide variety of models from Siamese cats to antelope and wild boar. The subjects included the following animals:

Badger, 3 inches
Brown Bear, 4 1/8 inches
Siamese Cat, (standing) 5 inches
Siamese Cat (lying) 3 3/4 inches
Langur Monkey, 4 3/8 inches
Pine Martin, 4¼ inches
River Hog, 3½ inches
Mountain Sheep, 5¼ inches
White-tailed Deer, 5 5/8 inches
Llama, 6½ inches
Nyla Antelope, 5 5/6 inches

These objets d'art never received popular recognition, and all the models are now discontinued except for the three Siamese cat figures. These are illustrated in color in the *Figure Collector's Book No. 13* and are still in current production. Although they were moderately priced when introduced, from $18.50 for the Pine Martin to $27.50 for the White-tailed Deer, The Chatcull animals are rare today and sell for over twice the price listed in the 1960 catalog.

Figures of calves, goats, and deer by Raoh Schorr were produced in limited editions in about 1936. Like the Chatcull animals, these were art sculptures and did not have a popular appeal. However they are valuable collectors' items, today, and are rare and hard to find.

Languar Monkey, HN 2657.

Siamese Cat, HN 2662 (lying).

Siamese Cat, HN 2660 (standing).

Hares. Large, HN 2593; small, HN 2594. (Collection Susan Kasulka.)

Persian Cat, white, HN 2539. Two-toned, HN 999.

Leopard on Rock, HN 2638. Height 9½ inches.

Sitting Tiger, HN 912, dated 1927. (Collection Mr. & Mrs. Robert M. Fortune.)

Penguin, L. HN 2633. Height 13 inches. (Courtesy Doulton & Co., Ltd.)

Llama, HN 2665.

Early Flambé animals. Top, crouching fox; bottom left to right: terrier dog, monkey, pig. (Collection Susan Kasulka.)

Sitting hound dog, HN 231, 8 inches. Same dog model in Flambé. (Collection Susan Kasulka.)

Royal Doulton
Flambé Animals
And Birds

Flambé elephant, HN 489 B. (Doulton & Co., Ltd.)

After years of experimentation with transmutation glazes, Doulton finally achieved success in about 1902. A collection of Flambé ware was first exhibited at the St. Louis World's Fair in 1904. Red was the predominate color in the early Flambé. There are also pieces with black and red and blue. A group of Flambé animals was illustrated in The *Connoisseur* in 1912. These included an elephant with trunk down, a hound dog, several figures of foxes, both sitting and lying down, a duck, a bird, a rabbit with one ear up, and a tiny mouse. There were also several group pieces; one of two piglets and one of two monkeys embracing. These animals are slightly stylized and are characterized by line design rather than realistic detail. The figures are small, from 2 to 4 inches. A group of three sparrows was 2 inches high by 3 inches wide. A Flambé group of two fan-tailed pigeons is 3 3/4 inches high, and a glazed red mouse sitting on a dark red cube is 2½ inches in height. An early group of two monkeys embracing is 2 3/4 inches high and is signed "Noke."

Group of Flambé animals. Top to bottom: Hare, ears down; hare, one ear up (early, HN 113); hare, sitting; two monkeys embracing, Noke model. (Doulton & Co., Ltd.)

Later Flambé animals include a large rhinoceros, 9½ inches, and a model of a bull, 10 3/4 inches, red with black markings. It is impressed-dated, 1930. An important owl figure measures 12 inches. A Flambé model of a leaping fish with red and black markings is also 12 inches high and is signed "Noke." A seated tigress, 6½ by 7 inches has the Doulton Flambé mark and the impressed date, April 1, 1929.

Charles J. Noke did not stop after his first Flambé, but continued to experiment and in 1920 he developed a new glaze which was called Sung. The Sung ware is characterized by blue flocculated markings. Many pieces of Sung are marked "Noke." A parrot, 15 inches, on a rock, has a blue glaze and a red head and breast. It is marked Sung and Noke. An elephant in Sung glaze with blue markings and a red head, 11 inches, has the Sung mark and is signed Noke. Another elephant figure with red and black markings is impressed 1930 and still another elephant figure, 6½ inches, has red, blue, and purple markings. In all, there were four elephant figures in Flambé and Sung. Three were listed in the 1950 Doulton catalogs and a fourth was listed in the catalog of January 1, 1959, and was priced $275.

The Flambé animals and birds listed in the 1950 catalogs are as follows:

Title	Number	Price
Ape	52	$8.00
Cat	9	12.00
Drake	137	26.50
Duck	112	4.50
Duck	395s/s	4.50
Elephant	489	37.50
Elephant	489A	30.00
Elephant	489B	22.50
Fox	14s/s	10.00
Fox	29	30.00
Fox	29A	12.00
Fox	29B	5.00
Fox	102	42.00
Guinea Fowl	69	15.00
Hare	119	8.00
Hare	656	13.00
Hare	656A	4.50
Hare	1157	9.00
Leaping Salmon	666	50.00
Mallard	654	26.50
Penguin	84	16.00
Penguin	239	26.50
Penguin	585	48.00
Penguin	1287	26.50
Pigs	61	30.00
Rabbit	113	4.50
Tiger	111	22.50
Tiger	809	52.50

Markings on early Flambé and Sung wares are as follows:

R.D.F. Royal Doulton Flambé

P.B.M. Standard Burslem mark printed with Flambé. P.F.M. added 1902 to 1930.

P.F.M. Printed Royal Doulton Flambé and script Sung, 1930 to present day.

Flambé Pekingese. (Collection Susan Kasulka.)

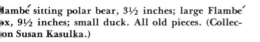

Flambé sitting polar bear, 3½ inches; large Flambé fox, 9½ inches; small duck. All old pieces. (Collection Susan Kasulka.)

Small elephant, small fox, c. 1950. (Doulton & Co., Ltd.)

Cock Pheasant. HN 2632. Height, 6¾ inches.

Royal Doulton
Bird Models

A salt-glazed stoneware figure of two cockatoos, 6 inches high, was modeled by Leslie Harradine and produced at Lambeth c. 1911-12. However, the bone china figures of birds that are the interest of collectors today were not produced until some years later. A group of sundry animals and birds listed in the Royal Doulton catalog, January 1, 1950, includes three figures of drakes and two miniature penguins. A Cock Pheasant, 2632, that was priced at $52.50 and a Mallard, 2635, priced at $60, were added to the list of birds in the catalog of January 1, 1959.

In addition to individual bird figures, a catalog of the late 1940s illustrates some decorative groups of birds in environmental settings. These include Kingfisher, HN 2541, 3 3/4 inches; Yellow-throated Warbler, HN 2546, 41/2 inches; Blue Bird, HN 2543, 5 3/4 inches; Duck, Mallard, HN 2555, 6 inches; Duck, Mallard, HN 2556, 41/4 inches; and a Chaffinch, HN 2550, 21/2 inches. Doulton also produced a Cock Pheasant, HN 2545, 71/2 inches, and a Hen Pheasant, HN 2610, 71/2 inches.

Large Tony Weller, mounted with music box. D no. 5531, 1936-1960. (Collection Ron Heberlee.)

IV. Character Jugs and Tobies

Royal Doulton Character Jugs and Tobies are one of the favorite interests of collectors today. Indeed the collecting of these jugs has become such a popular hobby that there are now many antiques dealers who specialize in Doulton jugs. The wide range of subject matter appeals to collectors of many different interests and hobbies and in various stations of life. The subjects range from characters taken from Dickens's novels and Shakespeare's plays to famous characters of English history and legend to traders and venders from the London streets. There are also characters from the world of sports such as the golfer, the jockey, and the yachtsman.

Although the majority of the subjects portrayed on the jugs relate to British interests, characters of American appeal such as Rip Van Winkle, the North American Indian, and Johnny Appleseed were added to the list of jugs as the jugs became popular. The historical series of Williamsburg included figures of the Gunsmith, the Guardsman, the Apothecary, the Gaoler, the Blacksmith, and the Bootmaker. The authenticity of these jugs is vouched for by Williamsburg Restoration, Incorporated.

Royal Doulton Toby and Character Jugs are twentieth century descendants of a long historical line of jugs fashioned in human likeness by potters from Egypt to those made in Britain during the Roman occupation and through the Middle Ages. But it was not until the mid-eighteenth century that the type known as the Toby Jug was first made by Ralph Wood and other Staffordshire potters.

The origin of the name Toby is obscure, but it seems to have been associated with conviviality from Elizabethan times, onward. There was the fat, jolly, Sir Toby Belch in Shakespeare's *Twelfth Night*. Then there was the character called Toby Philpot who was the subject of a popular song published in 1761. The early Toby was seated. He wore a three-cornered hat, a full-length coat, broad waistcoat, cravat, knee breeches, stockings and buckled shoes. In his left hand he generally held a jug and in his right hand a mug or a pipe. The early jugs were made so that each corner of the tricorn hat formed a spout for drinking.

John Doulton had produced portrait jugs of Nelson, Napoleon, and Wellington at the Lambeth Doulton pottery in the 1820s. Relief-decorated Toby wares with decoration of topers, hounds, and windmills had also been made at Lambeth. In 1875 the range of these wares was enlarged to include teapots, coffee pots, sugar bowls, cream pitchers, and condiment sets. As early as 1902, a small group of miniature Toby Jugs was made as bric-a-brac for cabinets. Also between 1924 and 1930, a series of jugs, tobacco jars and other shapes was modeled in a style similar to the eighteenth century tobies. These jugs, together with the Toby Jugs made in the Staffordshire potteries in the eighteenth and nineteenth centuries gave Charles J. Noke, chief designer at Royal Doulton Potteries, Burslem, 1914-1936, the idea of reviving the Toby and face-jugs. Noke's aim was to produce a series of original jugs representing popular characters from English legends, ballads, history, and literature designed to appeal to the present generation just as the original Toby Jugs did to preceding ones.

In about 1933, after months of experimenting in modeling, casting, and firing figures, Noke produced a jug that came up to his standards. Although the Doulton Character Jugs are descendants of the old Staffordshire Tobies, they have a style distinctly their own, and, although conceived in the same humorous and convivial spirit, they are more detailed than the earlier Toby and figure jugs. Also, where the original Tobies were depicted as seated figures, the Doulton Character Jugs designed by Noke show only the head and shoulders of the figure.

The first Character Jugs were produced by Charles J.Noke in 1934. They were John Barleycorn and Old Charley and they were instantly popular. These were followed in 1935 by Sairey Gamp, Parson Brown, Dick Turpin (with gun handle), Granny, and Simon the Cellarer. Jester, John Peel, Tony Weller, Touchstone, The Cardinal, and Vicar of Bray were produced in 1936. The next year, 1937, Paddy, Toby Philpot, and Mephistopheles, also known to present-day collectors as Two-faced Devil, were produced.

Doulton has put out a number of books illustrating Character Jugs, including the one published in 1955-1956 which illustrated in color all of the Character Jugs then in production and the seated Tobies and the Dickensware pitchers.

The earliest Character Jug book was a folder put out by Doulton c. 1952. It included John Barleycorn, John Peel, Parson Brown, Sairey Gamp, Toby Philpots, Paddy, Granny, Dick Turpin, Touchstone, Auld Mac, Vicar of Bray, The Cardinal, Simon the Cellarer, Mephistopheles, Farmer John, Old Charley, and Old King Cole. There was also a group of Dickensian characters including Mr. Pickwick, Fat Boy, Sam Weller, Tony Weller, Captain Cuttle, Sergeant Buz Fuz, and Mr. Micawber. A paragraph in the catalog reads: "These Jugs are modelled by a master hand, each subject being revealed by bold characterization. They are painted entirely by hand in most attractive colourings. Most are available in two sizes at very modest prices. Some are most effectively fitted with musical boxes which tinkle out a gay tune." A group of characters made into ash bowls was also illustrated. The ash bowls were introduced by Doulton in February, 1952. These include Auld Mac, Farmer John, Paddy, Sairey Gamp, Parson Brown, and Old Charley. These were discontinued in December, 1959. There were also ashtrays and stands with the characters Parson Brown, Old Charley, John Barleycorn, and Dick Turpin. These were also deleted in December, 1959.

The range of cigarette lighters included: Buz Fuz, Captain Cuttle, Mr. Pickwick, Old Charley, Long John Silver, Bacchus, The Lawyer, The Poacher, Captain Ahab, Beefeater, and Falstaff.

In June, 1953, Doulton introduced a series of small busts of Dickens characters. There were six characters: Mr. Micawber, Sairey Gamp, Sam Weller, Tony Weller, Mr. Pickwick, and Buz Fuz. These were discontinued December 31, 1959.

Charles J. Noke designed and modeled many of the Character Jugs. He was assisted by Harry Fenton who modeled figures, Character Jugs, and large presentation jugs at Doulton between 1928 and 1953. Max Henk and other Doulton modelers also modeled jugs. Cecil J. Noke, Charles Noke's son, was not a modeler, but he sketched many ideas for Character Jugs. Almost every year several jugs are withdrawn and new jugs added. In all there were over a hundred different Character Jugs.

The Character Jugs were produced in several sizes. Some were only made in large sizes; others in large and small, and quite a few were made in large, small, and miniature. Twelve were made in tiny size. The jugs made in tiny size were: 'Arry, 'Arriet, Auld Mac, Fat Boy, Cardinal, John Peel, Mr. Micawber, Mr. Pickwick, Old Charley, Paddy, Sairey Gamp, and Sam Weller. These "tinies" were all deleted in 1960.

The sizes of Character Jugs, according to Doulton & Company's *Collector's Book No. 5*, are as follows: large, 5¼ to 7½ inches; small, 3¼ to 4 inches; miniature, 2¼ to 2½ inches; tiny, 1¼ inches. Six jugs of Dickens characters were made in 1937 and 1939 in an odd size between large and small, about 4¼ inches. These were Buz Fuz, Capt. Cuttle, Fat Boy, Micawber, Pickwick, and Sam Weller. These were deleted in 1949.

From the standpoint of the serious collector, the most important Character Jugs are Mephistopheles and Clown. Mephistopheles or Two-faced Devil was introduced in 1937 and deleted shortly after World War II in 1948. On one side of the jug the Devil is shown with a gloomy expression, his mouth and mustache drooping. On the other side of the jug the face shows an alert, smiling expression with mustache and eyebrows pointed up. This jug was illustrated in the early Character Jug pamphlet but has never been shown in other jug books. It was made in large and small sizes. There are two clown jugs—Red-Hair Clown and White-Hair Clown. It is not known positively which jug was the original. Desmond Eyles, who was connected with the Doulton Lambeth factory for many years and whose book, *Royal Doulton, 1815-1962*, is a history of the Doulton Company, says: "As I recall, the Clown jug was originally introduced with red hair and it was not until recently that I discovered that it was also made with white hair." The Red-Hair Clown jug was introduced late in 1937 and deleted in 1942. It is of creamy white pottery with chin and cheek marks of red, black eyebrows, and orange-red hair. This is the most valuable of the two clown jugs. The White-Hair Clown was introduced in 1951 and deleted in 1955. The jug shows the head with white hair and pink face with white cheek and chin marks. The collar is red and the eyebrows are black. The clowns were only made in large size. The clown jugs were not illustrated in the Character Jug catalogs which leads one to surmise that few were made.

The jug of Field-Marshall Jan Christian Smuts of South Africa was issued in 1946 and deleted in 1948. Although there were few jugs made and these are hard to find, it is not the top favorite with American collectors.

The Pearly Boy is one of the rarest Royal Doulton Character Jugs. It is a version of 'Arry with buttons on the cap like the pearl buttons worn by the London Pearly Kings. The jug was made in all sizes from

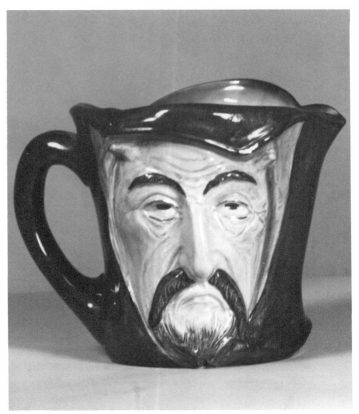

Front view, large size Mephistopheles. D no. 5757, 1937. Deleted 1948.

Back-view, Mephistopheles. (Collection Ron Heberlee.)

The Clown, Red: front view, no. 5610. 1937-1942.

The Clown, side view. (Collection Ron Heberlee.)

114

large to tiny. According to the Dennis catalog, a Pearly Boy and Pearly Girl were piloted but not put into production; however, the existence of both Pearly Boy and Pearly Girl jugs has been noted. These would be very rare.

A rare Churchill two-handled cup was modeled by Noke in 1940 and was probably deleted in 1941. The base has a printed inscription which reads: "Winston Spencer Churchill Prime Minister of Britain 1940. This Loving Cup was made during the Battle of Britain as a Tribute to a Great Leader." The cup was made only in large size.

The Character Jugs that are most in demand with American collectors are:

Mephistopheles
Red-Hair Clown
White-Hair Clown
Pearly Boy
Gladiator
Gulliver
'Ard of 'Earing
Punch and Judy Man
Simple Simon
Jan Christian Smuts
Gondolier

Right: Field-Marshall Smuts. Large. D no. 6198, 1946-1948. Inscription on base: "Field Marshall The Right Honourable J.C.Smuts, K.C.C.H., D.T.D. Prime Minister of The Union of South Africa and Commander in Chief of South African Forces." Left: Pearly Boy, small. Brown with red tie, pearl buttons on hat around visor and collar. Marked 'Arry. "A" mark. Very rare. D.no. 6235, 1947. (Collection Mr. & Mrs. Robert M. Fortune.)

Lord Nelson. Large. D no. 6336, 1952-1969. (Collection D.Shiaras.)

The Mikado. Large. D no. 6501, 1959-1969. (Collection D.Shiaras.)

The Vicar of Bray, Large. D no. 5615, 1936-1960. (Collection D. Shiaras.)

Touchstone. Large. D no. 5613, 1936-1960. (Collection D.Shiaras.)

Gladiator, Large. D no. 6550, 1961-1967. (Collection D.Shiaras.)

All Character Jugs were made at the Royal Doulton factory at Burslem. They were made in earthenware until 1968. From that time on they were made in fine, translucent china. Because Character Jugs are still being produced, it is important to know the markings so that the collector can determine whether a jug is old or new.

All Character Jugs with the exception of the tiny size are marked with the standard Royal Doulton trademark. When the jugs were introduced early in the 1930s, all of Doulton ware was fired in soft-coal-burning bottle kilns. Since they experienced difficulty in firing the jugs using the standard earthenware body, a special body was developed for the jugs and they were marked with the letter "A" c.1948. This was a factory control mark. In 1952 Doulton installed electric tunnel kilns and were then able to fire the jugs in the new kilns using the standard earthenware body. At which time, marking the jugs with the letter "A" was discontinued. After the "A" was discontinued, jugs were marked on the bottom with the Royal Doulton trademark with the name of the character beneath. Many of the "A"-marked jugs have the name in relief on the back of the character. "A" was not the first mark. The earliest jugs have the words "Reg applied for" or the registered design number. Beginning in 1960, current jugs were given an elaborate stamp with a series of registered numbers referring to world patents. Early jugs still in production such as Granny, Sairey Gamp, Auld Mac, Beefeater, Robin Hood, Monty, Drake, and Dick Turpin can be found with the "A" mark and earlier back stamps as well as the current mark. Most recent jugs have a number preceded by a "D" directly beneath the name of the character and the copyright numbers. It is not known when the "D" mark was first used.

The tiny jugs have their own mark—a circle formed by the words "Royal Doulton Made in England," with the name of the character in the center of the circle. The twelve characters made with this mark were discontinued in 1960. These tiny jugs are very rare, as are the jugs produced for a short time in the "special" size. The majority of the early jugs that were introduced in the 1930s have been discontinued, but some of the original characters are still being produced. There are also numerous variations in color and modeling, and some jugs still in production have undergone changes in detail and color.

Color changes were made in Drake in 1950. There is also an early version of Drake without a hat. In 1954 there was a color change in the Monty jug. There was also a color change in 'Arriet in 1951. The Nelson jug is often represented with a patch over the right eye, and the Cavalier had a collar change in 1950. Other minor changes in design included the change of the initials "G.R." to "E.R." when Queen Elizabeth II came to the throne in 1953. In 1949 the early version of Owd Mac was changed to Auld Mac. But the greatest changes were made in the two jugs, Dick Turpin and Robin Hood, both of which were deleted in 1960 and remade in new and different molds. The original Dick Turpin, which was produced in large, small and miniature sizes, is represented with a mask that is turned up on his hat, and the handle of the jug is a pistol. The new jug has the mask over his eyes and the handle of the jug is the head of a horse which is attached to the head of the character. The original Robin Hood jug has also been changed. Instead of a feather, the handle on the new jug is formed by a bow and a quiver of arrows. A bunch of oak leaves and acorns is attached to the hat which has a point in the front.

Now that production and withdrawal dates of all Royal Doulton Character Jugs are available, the collector can search with the assurance that he can find jugs with full authenticity. The search will only be limited by the amount of money available. If his purse allows he can search for the old, discontinued jugs. But some of these are hard to find and, since prices are high, the collector should learn as much as possible to avoid making mistakes. If his budget is low, he would do well to buy new jugs. These, too, are rising in price from year to year.

In addition to the information concerning marks and dates, a knowledge of the design of the jugs can also be of value in identifying the characters. For example, the shape and design of the jug handle is an aid in placing the age of jugs. The handles on early jugs such as John Barleycorn, Old Charley, Toby Philpots, Parson Brown, and the Vicar are simple utilitarian handles. However the handle of the Touchstone jug is in the form of a hooded-headed wand which is the badge of his jester's role. The form of this handle distinguishes this jug from the Jester jug.

From year to year jug handles became a more important part of the jug design, and the late jugs have handles which serve to identify the character depicted by the jug. The Johnny Appleseed jug has a handle in the form of a branch of the tree with a cluster of apples. The Gondolier handle represents the prow of a gondola; the handle of Scaramouche is a guitar with theatrical masks; the Punch and Judy Man handle is a small figure of Punch; the handle of St. George is a dragon; Long John Silver's handle is a parrot; the Merlin jug handle is an owl; and the Old Salt has the figure of a mermaid on the handle. The tiny figure of a dwarf sits in the handle of the Rip Van Winkle jug.

Since collectors frequently ask for information about the original characters who have inspired Royal Doulton Character Jugs, I have included a few brief notes giving the stories concerning the most important jugs.

The Dickensian Tobies and Character Jugs are some of the most interesting, mainly because of their association with Dickens's novels, and there is a large group of Dickens enthusiasts who collect these jugs. For those collectors who are not so familiar with the characters but fascinated by the jugs, the following sketches will give the stories of the jugs. The first Dickensian Character Jug was Sairey Gamp who was a character in Dickens's novel *Martin Chuzzlewit*. She was a gin-drinking, gossiping midwife who always carried a large bulging umbrella called a "Gamp" in England. Her character is realistically portrayed in the face of the jug which was created in 1935. Mr. Micawber was the incurable optimist from Dickens's *David Copperfield*. Although constantly out of work and out of money, he never despaired but always felt that something would "turn up." The jug, made in 1938, shows his jovial face with upturned mouth and smiling wrinkles.

Capt. Cuttle was the kindhearted sailor from Dickens's *Dombey & Son* who had a hook instead of a right hand. He always wears a hard-glazed hat.

Mr. Pickwick was from *The Pickwick Papers,* one of Dickens most popular books.

Fat Boy is also a character from *Pickwick Papers*. He is the Joe who is always eating or sleeping.

Samuel Weller, the faithful servant of Mr. Pickwick, is the center of the comic interest in *The Pickwick Papers*. He is a Cockney character of archness, shrewdness, and cunning which is all shown in the face of the mug.

Tony Weller is the father of Sam Weller. He drives a coach between London and Dorking. This inveterate philosopher wears a low-crowned hat with a broad brim.

Sergeant Buz Fuz is the lobster-complexioned bully—a low order of English barrister that has been abolished.

Mephistopheles is the character of the Devil from Goethe's *Faust* and Gounod's opera of the same name. The inscription on the small jug is from *Gargantua and Pantagruel* by Rabelais.

Gulliver is the figure of the traveler in the novel by Jonathan Swift. Although looked upon as a children's book it is really a social and political satire.

Scaramouche is a theatrical figure taken from the historical novel by

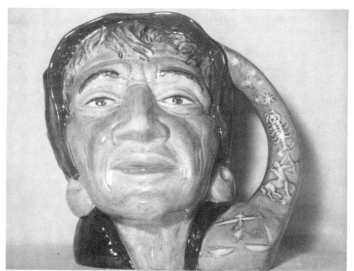

The Fortune Teller. Large. D no. 6497, 1959-1967.
(Collection D. Shiaras.)

Scaramouche. Large. D no. 6558. 1962-1967. (Collection D. Shiaras.)

The Cardinal. Large. D no. 5614. 1936-1960. Right:
Gondolier. Large. D no. 6589, 1964-1969. (Collection
Ron Heberlee.)

Regency Beau. Large. D no. 6559, 1962-1967. (Collection D. Shiaras.)

Gulliver. Large. D no. 6560, 1962-1967. (Collection
D. Shiaras.)

Raphael Sabatini dealing with the French Revolution.

The Ugly Duchess is a character from *Alice in Wonderland* by Lewis Carroll. The Duchess played croquet using a flamingo as a mallet; thus the jug handle represents a pink flamingo.

The Mikado was the Emperor of Japan and is also a character in the comic opera of that name by Gilbert and Sullivan.

Robin Hood is the outlaw hero of the Middle-Ages ballads whose chief haunt was the Sherwood Forest in Nottinghamshire. Friar Tuck was his companion and confessor.

Lord Nelson was the great British naval hero of the Battle of Trafalgar where he was fatally wounded in 1805.

Touchstone was the clown in Shakespeare's *As You Like It*. His jester's staff is the handle of the jug.

The Vicar of Bray was a semilegendary vicar of a well-known song written in English Restoration days.

The Cardinal is a red-robed dignitary of the Roman Catholic Church. He was popularized in the novels of Dumas.

John Barleycorn was the hero of many ballads. He is malt liquor, personified. An old song about John Barleycorn was written down by Robert Burns.

Simon the Cellarer was in charge of the wine cellar in Elizabethan days. His jug also suggests that he was also a taster.

Toby Philpots was the old potbellied character whose name was given to the first Toby jugs.

Dick Turpin was the notorious highwayman who was executed at York in 1739. He was the central figure in many legends and ballads.

Dick Whittington was a poor orphan boy who had nothing but a cat. He sent the cat to destroy the mice that troubled the King of Morocco. The king bought the cat, and with the money Whittington became wealthy and was thrice elected Lord Mayor of London.

The Fortune Teller represents the gypsy who follows her trade in English fairground booths.

Old King Cole and Simple Simon are figures from nursery rhymes.

John Peel is the character from the famous English hunting song "D' Ye Ken John Peel." The jug shows him in hunting attire and the handle is in the form of his hunting crop.

Uncle Tom Cobbleigh is the title of a Devon folk song in which this character and six cronies all ride to the Widdecombe Fair on Tom Pearse's gray mare.

The Cavalier represents a man who fought on the side of King Charles I in the civil war of the eighteenth century.

Parson Brown was the characteristic parson of the eighteenth century who was fond of drink and riding to the hounds.

Paddy is a typical Irish rogue. His face expressed the humor that is associated with the Irish.

Farmer John is the typical English farmer and Jarge is the typical country bumpkin.

Drake was the admiral of Queen Elizabeth's fleet that defeated the Spanish Armada.

Sam Johnson was a habitue of the London coffeehouses. He is famous for his *Dictionary of the English Language*.

Johnny Appleseed was a character in American folklore who traveled on foot across Pennsylvania, Ohio, Indiana, and Illinois planting apple trees.

'Arry and 'Arriet are Cockney street traders who sold their wares from wheelbarrows in London's Caledonian Market and Petticoat Lane.

The Gondolier was the singing boatman of Venice. There is a popular Gilbert and Sullian operetta called *The Gondoliers*.

The Town Crier is a figure from the Middle Ages. He walked the streets ringing a bell and shouting "Oyez" and giving the news of the day.

'Ard of 'Earing is a jug that represents a deaf man with his hand to his ear. The hand serves as the jug handle. Although a late jug, it was only in production from 1964 to 1967, so it is a good collectors' piece.

Regency Beau represents Beau Brummell whose elegance in dress was admired and imitated in nineteenth century England.

Captain Hook is the pirate captain in J.M. Barrie's *Peter Pan* who had a hook for a hand.

St. George is the patron saint of England. The legend of St. George and the dragon is the subject of an old ballad.

Viking. The Vikings were Norse pirates who invaded the coasts of England from the eighth to tenth century.

In addition to Character Jugs, Doulton made a series of full-figure, seated Toby Jugs. These were: Honest Measure, 4½ inches; Old Charley, 8 3/4 and 5½ inches; Happy John, 9 and 5½ inches; The Huntsman, 7½ inches; The Best Is Not Too Good, 4½ inches; The Squire, 6 inches; Double XX, 6½ inches; Jolly Toby, 6¼ inches; and a figure of Sir Winston Churchill made in three sizes, 9,5½ and 4 inches. There were also figures of Falstaff, 9½ and 6¼ inches, and a group of six smaller Tobies, 4½ inches high, of Dickens characters including Mr. Pickwick, Sam Weller, Sairey Gamp, Fat Boy, Mr. Micawber, and Capt. Cuttle. All of the seated Tobies were discontinued at one time, but production was resumed in 1973. The Tobies now produced and illustrated in the 1973 catalog are Huntsman, Honest Measure, Jolly Toby, Happy John, Falstaff, and Sir Winston Churchill.

'Arry. Large. D no. 6207, 1947-1960.

'Arriet. Large. D no. 6208, 1947-1960. (Collection D. Shiaras.)

In 1956, a full-figure Toby jug was made to order in two sizes for the American businessman, Cliff Cornell. The jugs were made in the likeness of Mr. Cornell in medium and small size. The figure is seated and wearing a brown suit. There is a cigar in his mouth and the figure is similar to the one of Churchill. The inscription on the bottom of the jug reads: "Greetings Cliff Cornell. Famous Cornell Fluxes Cleveland Flux Company" and the Royal Doulton trademark. It is not known how many of these Cornell jugs were made, but the jug is rare and would be an interesting addition to any jug collection.

The Character line of Doulton also included a series of tankards and square pitchers. The pitchers, 5½ inches tall, were decorated with scenes and characters from Charles Dickens's novels. The pitchers include: Old Curiosity Shop, Oliver Twist, Pickwick Papers, Old London, and the favorite with collectors, Old Peggotty. The name of the scene and a line from the book is often included in the decoration. The scenes are embossed and hand-painted in color underneath the transparent glaze.

The present-day cost of collecting the rare, eighteenth century tobies and the difficulty in finding them has turned the collector's interest to the

Left: CLIFF CORNELL. Large. Dark blue suit, white buttons and shirt, red tie, white dots, gray hat with black band, black shoes, cigar with pink end, diamond ring set in gold. Inscription on bottom: "Greetings Cliff Cornell. Famous Cornell Fluxes Cleveland Flux Company." **Right: THE SQUIRE,** seated Toby. Brown base, green coat, orange suit, brown hat, white hair, indents on top of hat for cigarettes. (Collection Mr. & Mrs. Robert M. Fortune.)

equally fascinating Royal Doulton Tobies and Character Jugs. The Doulton jugs bear comparison with jugs of earlier periods. Both are what is known as "popular art." However, the Royal Doulton Toby and Character Jugs have more detailed modeling than the eighteenth century Staffordshire jugs, and each Doulton jug is also hand-painted.

The main satisfaction of collecting is the enjoyment of the search and the excitement of finding the object. Although money may not be the chief consideration, the collector of Royal Doulton Tobies and Character Jugs has the satisfaction of knowing that the values are increasing from day to day. A comparison of dealers' advertisements gives concrete proof of this. Some jugs such as Mephistopheles and Clown are reaching the heights of high-priced collectibles.

A collection of Character Jugs can be started by visiting a china shop to see the new jugs. Such is the fascination of these jugs that it is hard to resist the urge to buy, and once one is the owner of a jug or two, he usually becomes a collector. This is the best way to start a collection of jugs, since the new ones soon increase in price. When one acquires more knowledge, it is time to start collecting the rare jugs.

Over fifty of the most important Character Jugs are no longer made. This makes them of special interest to the collector. The following is the list of the deleted jugs:

(1) John Barleycorn	1935......1960	
(2) Simon the Cellarer	1935......1960	
(3) Toby Philpots	1937......1969	
(4) Dick Turpin	1935......1960 (gun handle)	
(5) Dick Whittington	1953......1960	
(6) The Fortune Teller	1959......1967	
(7) Mr. Micawber	1938......1960	
(8) Capt. Cuttle	1938......1960	
(9) Fat Boy	1938......1960	
(10) Mr. Pickwick	1940......1960	
(11) Tony Weller	1936......1960	
(12) Sam Weller	1940......1960	
(13) Sergt. Buz Fuz	1938......1960 (small only)	
(14) Jester	1936......1960 (small only)	
(15) Touchstone	1936......1960 (L)	
(16) Old King Cole	1939......1960 (L & S)	
(17) Simple Simon	1953......1960 (L)	
(18) John Peel	1936......1960	
(19) Uncle Tom Cobbleigh	1952......1960	
(20) The Cardinal	1936......1960	
(21) The Cavalier	1940......1960 (L & S)	
(22) The Vicar of Bray	1936......1960 (L)	
(23) Parson Brown	1953......1960 (L & S)	
(24) The Clown	1937 . . . 1942-red (1951 . . . 1955-white)	
(25) Mephistopheles	1937......1948 (L & S)	
(26) Paddy	1937......1960	
(27) Jarge	1950......1960 (L & S)	
(28) Farmer John	1938......1960 (L & S)	
(29) Drake	1940......1960 (L & S)	
(30) Lord Nelson	1952......1960 (L & S)	
(31) Churchill	1940......1941 (L)	
(32) Sam Johnson	1950......1960 (L & S)	
(33) Field-Marshall Smuts	1946......1948	
(34) Johnny Appleseed	1953......1969	
(35) 'Arry	1947......1960	
(36) 'Arriet	1947......1960	
(37) Robin Hood (old model)	1947......1960	

(38) Friar Tuck	1951......1960
(39) Gondolier	1964......1969
(40) The Mikado	1959......1969
(41) Town Crier	1960......1973
(42) 'Ard of 'Earing	1964......1967
(43) Scaramouche	1962......1967
(44) Regency Beau	1962......1967
(45) Jockey	1971......1975
(46) Gladiator	1961......1967
(47) Gulliver	1962......1967
(48) Punch and Judy Man	1964......1969
(49) Ugly Duchess	1965......1973
(50) Capt. Hook	1965......1971
(51) St. George	1968......1975
(52) Viking	1959......1975

Group of small Character Jugs. Left to right: Farmer John, Cavalier, John Barleycorn, Toby Philpots, Drake. (Collection Ron Heberlee.)

Group of small Character Jugs, left to right: Beefeater, Sam Weller, Fat Boy, Micawber, Pickwick, Tony Weller. (Collection Ron Heberlee.)

The following is a list of jugs and their sizes in production today:

Anne Boleyn (L, introduced 1974)
Apothecary (L,S & M. 1956)
Aramis (L,S & M. 1956)
Athos (L,S & M. 1956)
Auld Mac (L,S & M. 1938)
Bacchus (L, S & M. 1959)
Beefeater (L,S & M. 1947)
Blacksmith (L,S & M. 1962)
Boot Maker (L,S & M. 1962)
Capt. Ahab (L,S & M. 1959)
Capt. Henry Morgan (L,S & M. 1958)
Catherine of Aragon (L. 1975)
Dick Turpin (Horse Handle) (L,S & M. 1959)
Don Quixote (L,S & M. 1957)
Falconer (L,S & M. 1950)
Falstaff (L,S & M. 1950)
The Gaoler (L,S & M. 1962)
Gardener (L, S & M. 1974)
Golfer (L. 1972)
Gone Away (L,S & M. 1961)
Granny (L,S & M. 1935)
The Guardsman (L,S & M. 1962)
The Gunsmith (L,S & M. 1963)
Henry VIII (L. 1975)
Izaak Walton (L. 1954)
Lawyer (L,S & M. 1959)
Lobster Man (L,S & M. 1968)

Long John Silver (L,S & M. 1952)
Lumberjack (L & S. 1967)
The Mad Hatter (L,S & M. 1965)
Merlin (L,S & M. 1960)
Mine Host (L,S & M.1957)
Monty (L. 1946)
Motorist (L,S & M. 1974)
Neptune (L,S & M. 1961)
Night Watchman (L,S & M. 1962)
North American Indian (L & S. 1968)
Old Charley (L,S & M. 1934)
Old Salt (L & S. 1961)
Pied Piper (L,S & M. 1954)
Poacher (L,S & M. 1955)
Porthos (L,S & M. 1956)
Rip Van Winkle (L,S & M. 1955)
Robin Hood (New model, bow handle.L,S & M.1960)
Robinson Crusoe (L,S & M.1960)
Sairey Gamp (L,S & M.1935)
Sancho Panza (L,S & M.1957)
The Sleuth (L,S M. 1974)
Smuggler (L & S. 1968)
Tam O'Shanter (L,S & M.1974)
The Trapper (L & S.1967)
Walrus and Carpenter (L,S & M.1965)
Yachtsman (L. 1972)

Ash bowls. Left: FARMER JOHN, brown hair, white collar, name impressed on back. Right: AULD MAC. Gray hair and beard, green hat. Indents for cigarettes and name impressed on back. (Collection Mr. & Mrs. Robert M. Fortune.)

The Poacher. Tans and green with red scarf.
Current. (Courtesy Doulton & Co., Ltd.)

'Ard of 'Earing. Large. D no. 6588, 1964–1967. (Collection Ron Heberlee.)

126

V. Artists Who Worked For Royal Doulton

Royal Doulton employed a large group of staff artists at both Lambeth and Burslem factories. The majority of them were not only experienced craftsmen but were also recognized artists. Among them were modelers and sculptors necessary for the modeling of the figures which Doulton produced from the early days, first at Lambeth, and then at Burslem. The best known modeler at Lambeth was the sculptor, George Tinworth. Tinworth had studied at the Lambeth School of Art. He had national recognition as a sculptor of religious subjects and was encouraged by John Ruskin.

From the beginning Doulton produced modeled figures. A catalog of 1887-1891 lists a humorous grotesque by Tinworth, also a group of sentimental terra-cotta statuettes including the nudes Morning and Evening. These nudes may have been designed by the sculptor-modeler John Broad who worked at Doulton Lambeth, 1873-1919. In 1883, Broad modeled a large, unglazed, buff terra-cotta figure, The Lambeth Potter. A few small copies of this figure were made for reproduction in 1903. The well-known, brown, salt-glazed stoneware figure of Queen Victoria, made in 1897 to commemorate her Diamond Jubilee, was also by John Broad. In 1902, a salt-glazed stoneware figure of the Boer War Soldier was modeled by Broad and in 1906 a dark gray, terra-cotta bust of William Pitt was produced to commemorate the centenary of Pitt's death. Broad also modeled a number of smaller, off-white decorative salt-glazed stoneware sculptures including the nude Girl and Lizard or The Bather and Atalanta. These were also made in porcelain, and a group of small, hard-paste bisque porcelain figures in period costume by Broad included Madame Pompadour, The Minuet, Doris Keane, and a pair of white Persian cats. These were made for reproduction in 1919-1921.

One of the most important modelers of Doulton figures was Arthur Leslie Harradine. Harradine worked at Lambeth from 1902 to 1914 and later at the Burslem factory from 1920 to 1960. In 1910 Harradine modeled busts of George V and Queen Mary in terra-cotta. These were stamped "Doulton Lambeth, L. Harradine Sc." Among Harradine's best-known figures were the bust of Charles Dickens made for the centenary of Dickens's birth in 1912, and the series of Dickens characters, including Sairey Gamp, Sam Weller, Mr. Pickwick, Fat Boy, Mr. Pecksniff, Mr. Micawber, and Uriah Heep. These were produced in light brown, dark brown, and white stoneware at Lambeth in 1912. In the same year Harradine designed and modeled spirit flasks with busts of the contemporary politicians, John Burns, David Lloyd George, Austin Chamberlain, Herbert Asquith, and Balfour. These flasks were produced in large editions, usually with Harradine's signature. There was also a figure-jug of

Mr. Pecksniff and a mug with relief figures of Dickens characters. Harradine also modeled a brown, salt-glazed stoneware figure of a French Legion soldier and two white-glazed figures of a Dutch Woman and A Toiler with blue-checked decoration. These were 7 3/4 and 8½ inches high and were made for reproduction. Other small figures by Harradine include Mother and Child, A Reaper, A Coalman, A Sower, Mermaids, Peasants, and a figure of two cockatoos. He also designed figures of dogs and other animals for reproduction at Burslem. Later Harradine modeled Beggar's Opera figurines and the figure of Owd Willum and The Poacher which were produced at Burslem. Harradine undoubtedly modeled other pottery and bone china figures that are at present unidentified.

Charles J. Noke began working for Doulton at Burslem in 1889. At first he modeled vases including the large pieces shown at the Chicago Exposition in 1893. However, Noke's real interest was in ceramic sculpture, and by 1894 he had begun to model figures. His earliest figures were of Henry Irving as Cardinal Wolsey, Ellen Terry as Queen Catherine and Mephistopheles and Marguerite. In 1897, Noke added the figures of The Jester, The Moorish Minstrel and Columbus. These were large figures from 10 to 20 inches high and were made in Parian. These figures were produced for reproduction in about 1919 and given HN numbers. In 1919, three figures, Digger, an Australian soldier (HN 322), Blighty, an English soldier of World War I (HN 343), and Canadian Mountie (HN 321) were made in a mottled, dark green glaze. The figures were 11½ inches high. The modeler is not identified, but he was probably Leslie Harradine. Also at about this time Noke, who was director of design at Burslem from 1914 to 1936, began to introduce the smaller bone china and earthenware figures.

Noke designed and modeled many of the figures, but he also had a large group of staff artists including designers, modelers and painters. One who assisted in modeling figurines besides Leslie Harradine was Harry Tittensor who worked at Burslem from 1900 to 1925. Tittensor was one of the most versatile artists who worked for Royal Doulton. In addition to painting figures and landscapes on vases and service plates, he designed figurines and large figure groups such as Europa and the Bull and Princess Badoura. Harry Fenton who was a modeler of tableware, figures, character jugs, and large presentation jugs worked for Doulton at Burslem from 1903 to 1911 and from 1928 to 1953. The artists who painted figurines included Harry Allen who worked on figurines from 1925 to 1950; Reginald Brown, a painter of flowers and landscapes who painted figurines from 1925 to 1962; William Edmund Grace who painted Series Wares, figurines and loving cups from 1902 to 1960; and Eric Webster who painted the figurines, animal, and bird models created by Charles Noke, the Champion Dogs modeled by Frederick T. Daws, and the horses modeled by W.M. Chance. Jack Roden painted large figure models such as St. George, and Harry Nixon was a general decorative painter. These artists were all experts in their field. The majority of them had been trained in such well-known potteries as Copeland, Worcester, Wedgwood, and Minton.

In addition to the staff artists on the regular payroll of the Doulton factories, Doulton employed independent modelers and sculptors such as members of the Royal Academy. This custom of employing the artistry of recognized artists helped to stimulate the factory artists to their best efforts. Doulton continues this custom down to the present day for their limited edition plates and wildlife figures.

The vogue for pottery and porcelain figures had a revival in England in the 1920s. This was due to two factors: first, the economic condition which restricted the size and number of rooms in the average dwelling; second, the conviction among the artists that art should aim to come within the scope of many rather than a privileged few. To this end several of England's foremost sculptors turned their attention to producing glazed pottery figures. Among these artists was the sculptor Charles Vyse.

KING CHARLES, HN 2084, 16½ inches high.
Noke model. Prestige Figure, (current).

Two folksy figures. Left: SILKS AND RIBBONS,
HN 2017. Right: OWD WILLUM, HN 2042. Model
by Leslie Harradine. (Courtesy Doulton & Co., Ltd.)

Charles Vyse became well known for his ceramic sculpture. Vyse was a native of the pottery district and was descended from a family of Staffordshire workers in clay. However Vyse also studied at the Royal College of Art and worked as a sculptor for many years and his work in this field was well known to the public from his large figures exhibited at the Royal Academy. In about 1920 Vyse abandoned sculpture on a large scale for work in glazed and painted earthenware. Vyse used a white pottery body fired at high temperature and the decoration was painted in colors, mostly applied before glazing. The number of individual models was limited since the molds lasted for only twelve or fifteen castings before they lost their sharpness. To obtain satisfactory results a statuette is built up of numerous separate molds so that the seam lines will not show. The several versions of any model are capable of varied colorings. Most of the Vyse's figures were about 10 inches in height. The subjects were from the life in the London streets. There is a figure of the balloon woman, the lavender girl, and a woman with a basket of tulips. Although Doulton produced other similar figures, they were not designed by Vyse, but they certainly show his influence. However, Vyse did create three figures for Doulton as early as 1913. The small figure, HN 1, Darling, a little figure of a boy in his nightgown which has proved popular through the years and is still in production and Elizabeth Fry were produced at this time. The Return of Persephone was designed for Doulton in 1911 and was produced in china at the Burslem factory. It was given the number HN 1 and has been discontinued for many years.

Phoebe Stabler was another of England's foremost sculptors who turned her talents to glazed pottery figurines. Her most important themes were childhood and fairies. Phoebe Stabler was employed to model an early group of small figures for Royal Doulton. The figures were produced at Burslem. They included Milking Time, HN 3; Picardy Peasant (female, blue, HN 4); Picardy Peasant (female, gray, HN 5); Picardy Peasant (male, blue, HN 13); Picardy Peasant (male, green, HN 19); Madonna of the Square (mauve, HN 10). This figure was also made in dark blue, gray, and gray and green. The figure is still in production. The Lavender Woman, (HN 22), also by Phoebe Stabler, was made in several different colorings, as was the figure of Sleep (HN 24). The figure of Sleep has long been out of production and is thus a rare figure for the collector.

Other early figurines designed by nonstaff artists were Crinoline, HN 8, by George Lambert; A Lady of the Georgian Period, HN 41; and A Lady of the Elizabethan Period, HN 40, by E.W. Light. The Sleepy Scholar, HN 15; The Attentive Scholar, HN 26; and The Coquette, HN 20, by William White, were figures of small children made in about 1912. Blacker saw these figures and also the figure Jester by Noke. He reports his visit in an article in The *Conoisseur* in 1912 as follows: "I must call your attention to the group of three coloured figures exquisitely modeled by William White, a fellow-student of Sir Thomas Brock. These are worthy of all praise reproducing perfectly the spirit of the old Staffordshire style."

Blacker also gives a picture of the workrooms at the Burslem factory. "I visited a work-room where the youngest painters and decorators were actively pursuing their vocation. With what skill, what rapidity, and what perfect accuracy the work grew under the facile fingers of even the youngest . . . painters, gilders and decorators in one large studio. The well-known painters had their separate studios."

The noted sculptor, Richard Garbe, R.A., Principal of the School of Sculpture at the Royal College of Art, modeled a number of vases and ceramic sculptures for Doulton in the 1930s. A salt-glazed Doulton Ware vase with amber-colored glaze having nude figures in relief; a brown stoneware vase with figures of boys and girls; and a stoneware bottle with figures of Endymion and Aurora were made at Lambeth. Garbe also modeled several figures of seals and sea lions that were produced with a bronze glaze. There was also a green and brown stoneware flower vase with a kneeling figure of a nude in glazed white stoneware.

A group of statuettes by Richard Garbe was produced in a special china-clay body with a slightly tinted matt glaze. These were produced in limited editions of 25 to 100. These sculptures were from 15 to 26 inches high. They include Spring, a slender, draped figure, 20 inches high, which was made in an edition of 100 with each piece bearing the sculptor's signature and number. The figure was illustrated in a Doulton catalog of the 1930s. Other figures by Richard Garbe include: Spirit of the Wind, West Wind, Lady of the Snows, Lady of the Rose, and a smaller figure, Salome. These figures were all given HN numbers. A porcelain head of Beethoven from the original sculpture that had been exhibited at the Royal Academy in 1931, was produced by Doulton in an edition of 25. It has the Burslem script marks. Garbe also designed a number of porcelain wall masks that were produced by Doulton in editions of 100. The masks included Fate, Lion of the East, and St. Agnes. St. Agnes was produced in several different colorings, including a turquoise glaze. All of the Garbe figures and masks are rare collectors' pieces.

Gilbert Bayes, an architectural sculptor known for heroic equestrian bronzes, also did smaller work in pottery and wood. In 1925, Bayes executed stoneware figures in colored glazes for a child-fountain. A copy of the fountain made in pottery was set outside the British Pavilion at the Paris Exhibition in 1925. Bayes' panel, *Pottery Through the Ages*, was erected over the main entrance of Doulton House on the Albert Embankment in 1939. Bayes died in 1953 after an association with Doulton of over thirty years.

Among the other nonfactory artists whose work was reproduced by Royal Doulton was Reco Capey, an industrial designer. His pieces were fired at Lambeth in the 1930s and have the Lambeth stamp and his signature. The pieces did not appeal to the public but are rare collectors' items today.

Kruger Gray, Allan Howes, Alexander J. Marshall, George Paulin, and James Woodford were among other modelers and sculptors whose designs were reproduced by Doulton. Donald Maxwell did designs for Doulton tiles and the well-known painter, Frank Brangwyn designed vases and tableware that were produced at Doulton's Burslem factory. Some of this ware was signed, "Designed by F. Brangwyn Royal Doulton England," and other pieces were marked "Brangwyn Ware" with the standard Burslem trademark.

The artist Raoh Schorr designed models of goats and sheep which were produced in limited editions by Doulton. These are now rare collectors' items.

The well-known water color artist Cecil Aldin furnished sketches of terrier dogs which were adapted for use by Noke, and between 1929 and 1939 Doulton Burslem produced a whole series of items including rack plates, cups and saucers, ashtrays, etc. The series was entitled "Aldin's Dogs." The pieces were decorated with whimsical color sketches of dogs chasing their tails, chewing slippers, yawning, smoking pipes, etc. Each piece had a reproduction of the artist's signature. Aldin wrote and illustrated many books about dogs. In 1927, *Dogs of Character* by Cecil Aldin was published by Charles Scribner's Sons. The illustrations in the book are similar to Doulton's Dogs of Character and the Doulton dog figures were inspired by Aldin's illustrations, but Aldin never actually modeled any of the Doulton figures of dogs.

The artist Peggy Davies is one of the best known porcelain sculptors in England. Mrs. Davies has been associated with Doulton for almost thirty years. She modeled the Royal Doulton Matador and Bull, Indian Brave, some of the Championship Dogs, and figures of Williamsburg. In 1970 Mrs. Davies began modeling the figures of the Lady Musicians limited edition, which was just completed in 1976.

Bibliography

Blackner, J.F. Articles from The *Connoisseur* (1911-1912).

Dennis, Richard. *Lambeth Art Pottery*. London: The Hillington Press, 1975.

_____. *Doulton Stoneware Pottery, 1870-1925*. London: Robert Stockwell Ltd., 1971.

_____. *Character Jugs*. London: Malvern Press, 1976.

Doulton & Company, Ltd. *Figure Collectors Catalogues*, vols. 1-8.

Eyles, Desmond. *Royal Doulton, 1815-1965*. London: Hutchinson, 1965.

_____. *The Doulton Lambeth Wares*. London: Hutchinson, 1975.

_____. *Good Sir Toby*. London: Doulton & Co., 1955.

Stables, Mrs. Gordon. "Vogue of Figurines Revived." *International Studio,* May, 1923, vol. 77.

_____. "The Pottery Figures of Mr. Charles Vyse." *International Studio,* May, 1923, vol. 77.

Index

Subject Index

Index to Pieces

137